TWAYNE'S WORLD AUTHORS SERIES

A Survey of the World's Literature

Sylvia E. Bowman, Indiana University

GENERAL EDITOR

JAPAN

Roy E. Teele, University of Texas at Austin

EDITOR

Kōda Rohan

TWAS 432

Kōda Rohan

KŌDA ROHAN

By CHIEKO IRIE MULHERN
University of Illinois, Urbana

TWAYNE PUBLISHERS
A DIVISION OF G. K. HALL & CO., BOSTON

895.63
K76 M
1977

Library of Congress Cataloging in Publication Data

Mulhern, Chieko.
    Koda Rohan.

    (Twayne's world authors series ; TWAS 432 : Japan)
    Based on the author's thesis, Columbia, 1973.
    Bibliography: pp. 169–73
    Includes index.
    1. Kōda, Rohan, 1867–1947—Criticism and interpretation.
PL810.03Z75   895.6′3′4   76–50541
ISBN 0–8057–6272–8

Contents

About the Author

Chieko Irie Mulhern was born and raised in Japan, where she attended Aoyama Gakuin University, before coming to the U. S. in 1959. She graduated from Brooklyn College of the City University of New York with a bachelor's degree in English literature, and received her master's degree and doctorate in Japanese literature from Columbia University.

She taught Japanese at Princeton University from 1970 to 1974. She is Assistant Professor of Japanese Literature and Language at the University of Illinois (Urbana, Illinois), teaching courses in Japanese literature, culture, and cinema.

Her master's thesis was published as *"Otogi-zōshi*: Short Stories of the Muromachi Period," *Monumenta Nipponica* (Summer, 1974). Her translation works include an *otogi-zōshi* tale "Princess Flower Spirit"; "The Five-storied Pagoda" and "Encounter with a Skull" by Kōda Rohan; and autobiography of Hani Motoko. Currently she is engaged in research on Higuchi Ichiyō with the focus on the female conflict in Japanese literature.

Preface

I have experienced three serious value crises in my life. The least drastic was the third—when my personal circumstances necessitated adjustment to American values without renunciation of my native traditions. The first was a collective crisis, a national trauma, which constituted a thorough, cataclysmic annihilation of faith in the irrevocability of any value system. The Japanese of my own generation and older have never to this day fully recovered from the searing memories of the days immediately following the summer vacation of 1945. In every elementary school classroom, we sat with a writing brush dipped in black ink, obliterating in our textbooks passage after passage as the teachers tearfully declared them mendacious and iniquitous according to the directives issued by a mystical authority in the name of General Douglas MacArthur. Until a new set of "uncorrupted and factual" textbooks were distributed, we pupils lived with the old ones which we had been taught to love and cherish and then inexplicably ordered to mutilate with our own hands—a visual proof of the humiliating defeat and an indelible scar of skepticism.

In terms of its impact on my emotional constitution and character formation, nevertheless, the most devastating was the second, a bitterly personal crisis. After the war, I was adopted by my stepfather, who held a pertinacious conviction that a girl need study only practical sciences helpful in her future role as a household engineer, avoiding at all costs the contaminating effect of literature (by nature immoral and corrupting without a shred of redeeming merit). Driven by an irrepressible craving for knowledge, I took to borrowing three books a day from a local library to read at night, burying myself and a lamp under a quilted cover. Within two years, I read books on all subjects from one end of the modest library to the other, but by then my inner conflict was mounting to an unbearable intensity.

I was overwhelmed by a sense of guilt over my secret, ungrateful defiance of my stepfather, who was bringing me up through a period of unprecedented national hardship and material privation; my wicked, accursed infatuation with books; and a nagging suspicion that my own beliefs might not be totally reprobate. More importunate, however, was my increasing despair in a search for absolute values that would unequivocally clarify the ambiguity of right and wrong forever.

It was at this point in my life and at the age of fifteen that I encountered a short story which dispelled my pessimism and altered my outlook on life. It made me realize that the absolute values did indeed exist without invalidating all contradictory values. It taught me to accept the paradoxical truth that love can sometimes hurt its object even when it is genuine and that my disobedient search for knowledge would not expunge my filial piety. The story was the "Encounter with a Skull" and the author was Kōda Rohan.

In the history of modern Japanese fiction, there is a period often referred to as the *Kōro jidai*. *Kō* designates Ozaki Kōyō (1867–1903), the leader of the Kenyūsha literary group and the master storyteller most responsible for the popularity of Japanese neoclassicism (*Gikotenshugi*). *Ro* represents a writer of idealistic fiction, Kōda Rohan (1867–1947). The term *Kōro jidai*, or the Age of Kōyō and Rohan, is loosely applied to the Meiji twenties (1887–1897), when these two writers of the same age produced the bulk of their fiction; but more precisely, it covers the period between 1889 (when Rohan made his literary debut) and 1903 (the year of Kōyō's death and Rohan's last attempt in pure fiction).

The significance of this period is multiple. It was about this time that modern Japanese literature attained a degree of maturity for the first time. By the Meiji Restoration of 1868, Japanese literature had approached its most stagnant stage— hopelessly ribald, sentimental, unoriginal, and inconsequential. In the 1870s and the early 1880s, however, translated Western works such as *Robinson Crusoe*, *The Arabian Nights*, and Jules Verne's early science fiction stimulated Japanese imagination and unfolded new literary horizons. And the fervent political consciousness of the late 1880s generated a new genre, the political novel, of expansive scale though limited by its primarily didactic purpose of popular enlightenment. Following such literary trends, Futabatei Shimei (1864–1909) heralded the birth of modern Japanese literature with his novel, *Ukigumo* (1887–1889), which was inspired by Russian realism; this novel contained characters with depth, a meticulous psychological study of individual ego, and was a successful adaptation of the spoken language into literature. Along with Futabatei, Rohan and Kōyō played a crucial role in the evolution of truly creative literature of the Meiji Japan.

The Age of Kōyō and Rohan betokens a successful alternative to, or even an inevitable departure from, the literary proclivities of the preceding hundred years, bitterly denounced by Tsubouchi Shōyō (1859–1935, the first modern literary critic in Japan) as being either excessively frivolous or rigidly didactic. Shōyō expounded the need for a new literature of intrinsic value as well as the use of realistic techniques from Western fiction. While Futabatei responded with his *Ukigumo*, Kōyō contributed superior genre novels inspired by the realistic slice-of-life tales of the rediscovered Japanese writer Ihara Saikaku (1642–1693); and Rohan expanded the potential of literature with his stories charged with poetic passion and philosophical insight.

The neoclassical literature of Kōyō and Rohan championed, if unwittingly, the nationalistic revival of classical literature and native Japanese culture—a popular reaction against the government-imposed precipitate Westernization movements. In their inclination toward a predominantly East Asian literary tradition, Kōyō and Rohan remain unique among the major writers of modern Japanese literature, the mainstream of which has been for the most part Western oriented.

This volume is the first comprehensive study of Rohan's life and works in English. Its primary aim is to provide the following: (1) a brief biographical background helpful in understanding Rohan's fiction; (2) a chronological discussion of his major works, focusing on literary techniques and themes; and (3) an introductory exploration of Rohan's complex idealism as reflected in his stories, drawing from minor works and scholarly treatises as well.

It is not within the scope and intent of this volume to delve deeper into the erudite philosophical and religious concepts (such as *ālaya vijñāna* and the principle of emptiness) beyond the extent to which they have direct relevance to an understanding of Rohan's own writings or of the popular beliefs of his contemporary Japanese and to which they call attention to Oriental sources that might be cumbersome for the Western reader to trace. Similarly, literary analysis by Western critical methods and comparison with Western fiction are kept to a minimum in the hope that translations of Rohan's works will soon provide an opportunity for the reader to apply such comparative approaches.

This book was originally written at Columbia University as my doctoral dissertation, "Kōda Rohan: A Study of Idealism" (1973). I wish to thank Professor Donald Keene not only for his guidance and invaluable suggestions without which this book might have remained my reverie but, more profoundly, for the perpetual inspiration and encouragement I derive from his works. For the initial preparation of the biographical chapter, I am indebted to Professor Marleigh Ryan, currently of the University of Iowa. I am grateful to Professor Yoshito Hakeda of Columbia University for his advice particularly in regard to Buddhist concepts. No word of gratitude could fully express my appreciation of the meticulous editorial assistance and insightful advice I received from my editor, Professor Roy E. Teele. I am, however, solely responsible for any errors and naive assumptions found in this book.

The Council for International and Regional Studies of Princeton University provided me with an airfare to Japan in the summer of 1973, making additional research possible. My deep gratitude goes to Ms. Soowon Y. Kim and Ms. Mariko Shimomura, the Japanese catalogers at Gest Oriental Library of Princeton University, who continuously supplied the latest publications and references with astonishing alertness and expertise. I wish to thank my husband, Arthur Mulhern, for his patience, cooperation, and understanding during the long period of research and writing of this book. I am deeply thankful to Mr. and Mrs. Ronald Kronheim and Mr. and Mrs. Jerome Kronheim, who sponsored my coming from Japan to the United States as an undergraduate student. Lastly, I would like to express my love and respect for the most courageous ladies I have known, my grandmother and my mother, to whom this first book of mine is dedicated.

C<small>HIEKO</small> I<small>RIE</small> M<small>ULHERN</small>

University of Illinois, Urbana

Chronology

1867   Kōda Shigeyuki born on the twenty-third day of the lunar seventh month in Edo (present-day Tokyo).

1872   Begins education in a private school.

1875   Enters Ochanomizu Grade School.

1879   Enters Tokyo First Middle School.

1880   Withdraws from Middle School and begins to frequent the Tokyo Library.

1881   Enters Tokyo English School.

1882   Withdraws and attends a private school of Chinese learning.

1883   Enters Telegraphers Training School. Begins to write Chinese poetry and philosophical discourses.

1885   Assigned to telegraph office in Hokkaido.

1887   Leaves post and returns to Tokyo, prompted by literary ambition.

1889   Makes successful literary debut with "Dewdrops," under the pen name, Rohan. Writes "Love Bodhisattva" and "A Rare Man."

1890   Publishes "Encounter with a Skull," "Venomous Coral Lips," "A Sword," and "A Sealed Letter." Accepts an associate staff novelist appointment at the *Kokkai* Newspaper.

1891   Publishes "The Wandering Balladeer," "Surprise Gunshot," and the novel *The Whaler*. Wins critical acclaim with the serialized "The Five-storied Pagoda."

1893   Begins serial novel, *The Minute Storehouse of Life*.

1894   Terminates *The Minute Storehouse of Life* due to a serious illness and the Sino-Japanese War.

1895   Marries Yamamuro Kimiko. Publishes "New Urashima."

1896   Begins secondary career as literary critic by reviewing current fiction works and editing fiction magazine, *Shin Shōsetsu*. Publishes "The Bearded Man."

1898   Publishes "This Day" and "Demon of Love."

1899 "Kyūbei the Potter."
1901 "That Day."
1903 Begins *Waves Dashing Against Heaven*. His daughter Aya born.
1905 Composes a long poem, *Leaving the Hermitage*. Writes "Clay Image, Wooden Image."
1908 Appointed Lecturer of Japanese Literature at Kyoto Imperial University.
1909 "The Five-storied Pagoda" translated into English as *The Pagoda* and published in Tokyo. Resigns from the university position and returns to Tokyo.
1910 Death of his wife Kimiko.
1911 Awarded a doctorate in literature.
1912 Marries Kodama Yayoko.
1913 A play, *Nawa Nagatoshi*, staged at Tokyo Imperial Theater.
1919 Death of his mother. Publishes "Destiny."
1925 London publication of his poem translated as *Leaving the Hermitage*. Writes "Viewing of a Painting."
1945 Death of his second wife.
1947 Completes commentaries on Bashō's poems. July 30, Rohan dies of pneumonia.

CHAPTER 1

Family and Early Life

I *The Kōda Family*

KŌDA Rohan was born in the Kanda district of Edo (re-named Tokyo in 1868) on the twenty-third (or twenty-sixth) day of the seventh month in 1867, the last year of the Edo period. Rohan himself did not know the exact date of his birthday, because the lunar calendar was replaced by the current New Style Calendar in 1872; but he preferred the twenty-third. In accord with the custom of the samurai class, he was given a childhood name, Tetsushirō (*"shirō"* designating the fourth son), as well as the legal name, Shigeyuki. Rohan is the pen name by which he is best known.

Rohan's mother, Yū (1842?–1919), was the only child of Kōda Ritei, who held the hereditary position of *omote bōzu*, a Shogunate official in charge of protocol, ceremonies, audience appointments, and such. Called *bōzu* ("monk") because of his shaven head, an *omote bōzu* was nonetheless a samurai serving directly under the Shogun. In addition to the annual stipend of forty bushels of rice, Ritei owned real estate proper-ties which had been granted by the Shogun and which yielded an annual rent of about two hundred *ryō*. (In the late Edo period, one *ryō* could buy one *koku* of hulled rice, which was sufficient to feed one adult for a year. Forty Japanese bushels equaled approximately sixteen *koku*. A servant was paid from 2.5 to 4 *ryō* a year.)[1] Ritei received, moreover, summer and year-end gratuities from numerous *daimyo* (feudal lords) and Shogunate officials, totalling one hundred *ryō*. Since the daily duties of *omote bōzu* involved direct contact with the *daimyo*, high-ranking officials, and even the Shogun himself at times, Ritei exercised considerably more influence in reality than his relatively small official stipend would indicate. When

15

Rohan was born, the Kōda family was residing in a house
with an impressive gate reflecting their affluence and social
status.

According to the recollections of Rohan's daughter, Rohan's
mother was a sternly dignified lady with a tranquil yet un-
approachable air about her. Rohan held his mother in awe,
always addressing her in the most honorific terms. He once told
his daughter an anecdote of his childhood which illustrates his
mother's stoic attitude. One winter day when Rohan was still
a small child, his mother found the boy with his hands hidden
inside his kimono sleeve for warmth. She led him to a wooden
pillar and urged him to warm his hands by hitting them
against the pillar rather than hiding them.[2] Rohan never again
permitted himself to relax in such an inelegant posture. Yū is
said to have been exceptionally gifted in calligraphy and traditional Japanese music. She was to produce, in addition to
prominent sons, two daughters who became first-rate musicians.

Rohan's father, Shigenobu (1839?–1914), was the son of an
oku bōzu, with similar duties but lower in rank than *omote
bōzu*. He married Yū and took her family name. "He was quite
learned and cultured for a samurai of the time. Very sincere
and steadfast, he was also a sensitive Edoite with a talent
for writing and a taste for music."[3] When the abdicated Shogun's
heir moved from Edo to his new fief in Shizuoka in July, 1868,
the Kōda family did not accompany the Tokugawa lord, thereby
forfeiting its stipend and hereditary position. Shigenobu became
a minor official in the Ministry of Finance, but his position
was among many that were abolished in 1885 in the course of
an extensive reorganization of bureaucratic structure. He appears to have been a man of fervent beliefs and a passionate
nature. Moved by the inspirational lectures delivered by Uemura
Masahisa (1857–1925, the most influential Protestant minister
of the Meiji period),[4] Shigenobu relinquished Nichiren Sect
Buddhism, which had been the hereditary family faith, to have
himself and members of the family baptized as Christians around
1886. Rohan, who was away in Hokkaido at the time, was the
only exception. When his second son settled in the bleak Kurile
Islands, Shigenobu, despite his old age, joined him for a time
after 1900 to live in the Shumushir Island settlement.

Rohan was usually reticent on the subject of his own family, but in response to a magazine questionnaire of 1903 he named five great contemporary figures: "Emperor, Empress, Crown Prince, my father, and my mother" (XL, 193). Whether the first three were cited merely out of conventional consideration (rather unlikely for a man so independent in his thought) or out of truly patriotic loyalty, one cannot say. As for his parents, however, he added: "People may consider my parents not worthy to be named here. But for myself, I cannot help but feel the greatness of my parents. Beside them, all others are merely my seniors, my peers, or my juniors, none great enough to impress me with the strength of their character" (XL, 193). Such respect for his parents seems more than justified in light of the honors and fame brought to the Kōda family by their offspring, beyond what any one family could normally expect. In 1900, someone under the pseudonym, Yōdō Koji, expressed the widely shared admiration in a literary news column, listing the brilliant accomplishments of the Kōda children.[5]

The second son, Shigetada (1860–1924), married into an heirless *omote bōzu* family and, taking his wife's family name, came to be known in history as Gunji Taii (naval Lieutenant Gunji), the famed organizer and leader of Hōkōgikai (Association of Patriotic Services). This brother in a sense personified what would later emerge as Rohan's ideal hero. In 1893, Gunji resigned from active duty to lead his Hōkōgikai members to the northernmost island of the Kuriles. Their departure was marked by a spectacular farewell. Fireworks were exploded, and the naval band played Auld Lang Syne joined by thousands of well-wishers lining the banks of the Sumida River. From the viewing stand, the official speech was delivered by Viscount Tani Kanjō (1837–1911, the heroic commander who had successfully defended the Kumamoto Castle during the Seinan Rebellion of 1877). Rohan, who accompanied his brother aboard a boat to Yokosuka, recounts the experience in the postscript to the *Biography of Gunji Shigetada* (1939) by Captain Hirose Hikota: "Approaching the port of Yokosuka, we noticed a number of battleships whose masts and riggings were completely covered with crewmen. Learning that it was called the main rigging salute, I turned my face down, unable to control my surging tears" (XXX, 503). Gunji's departure scene is depicted in many paintings. At about the same time, an army Colonel Fukushima was on his lone trek on horseback across the Euro-Asiatic Continent. The nation enthusiastically followed the progress of the two parties as if it were a navy-army competition, and there even appeared a new backgammon game called the expedition *sugoroku* of Lieutenant Gunji and Colonal Fukushima.[6] Advocates of the national essence movement (*kokusuishugi*) hailed Gunji as a champion of a patriotic, positive idealism.[7]

A monument raised in 1937 by the Kita Chishima Chamber of Fisheries on Gunji Hill in Shumushir Island paid tribute to Lieutenant Gunji:

You deeply lamented the fact that our remote areas were neglected and left to serve as bases for poaching foreign vessels. . . . You organized Hōkōgikai of two hundred seventeen Kurile development settlers. Honored by the grant from the Imperial Privy Purse, you set out on a long perilous voyage in small boats on March 20, 1893, and developed Shumushir and other islands. For many years you endured hardship and held to the northern Kuriles, establishing fishing bases, further exploring the geography and ocean resources along the continental coast line, thereby contributing to the security of our national rights and interests. Our vast fishery industry in the northern waters owes its beginning entirely to you.[8]

Later in 1904, when the Russo-Japanese War broke out, Gunji landed in Kamchatka with nineteen members and erected two sign posts, one in Japanese and the other in English, proclaiming the area to be a Japanese territory. Gunji and Dr. Oda Naotaro (a friend of Rohan's) were captured by the Russians, and Gunji was imprisoned in Petropavlovsk. While Ambassador Komura Jutarō was attending the Portsmouth peace conference, Gunji sent him a letter by favor of an American ship's captain, advocating the crucial importance of Japanese northern territories. This letter is said to have helped shape item seven of the peace treaty. Rohan was so severely affected by his brother's perils that he was unable to continue his newspaper serial novel, even after Gunji's safe return at the end of the war. During World War I, Gunji was dispatched to Siberia on a secret mission. Rohan ardently admired this brother, whose image is indirectly but deeply imprinted in the Rohanesque hero type.[9]

Such aggressive, though never mercenary, activism exemplified by Gunji's career was also prominent in Rohan's two sisters. Nobuko (1870–1946) received music instruction from Luther Whiting Mason[10] in Tokyo during her childhood; and she was the first music student on government scholarship to study in Boston (1890–1891) and Vienna (1891–1896). Mori Ōgai (a novelist friend of Rohan's) wrote a short article in 1896 ecstatically rejoicing that with Miss Kōda's return from abroad "an authentic taste in Western music [namely, Mozart and Beethoven] was finally established in Japan."[11] Nobuko's brilliant professional skill as a pianist and her dynamic leadership in the music world[12] earned her a nickname, Dowager Empress (Seitaikō) of the Ueno Music School, where she taught. When the Imperial Academy of Arts (Teikoku Geijutsu In) was established in 1937, Nobuko was nominated in the field of music together with her brother Rohan in literature.

The younger sister, known by her married name Andō Kōko (1878–1963), studied in Berlin under Joseph Joachim from 1900 to 1904. In 1932, she was invited to Vienna as a judge in an international music contest and stayed for ten months. An accomplished violinist and a professor of the Tokyo (formerly Ueno) Music School, Kōko was a music tutor to the Crown Princess (the present Empress Nagako) for a time, while her sister Nobuko taught the Empress Takako (of the Emperor Taishō). Apparently, Rohan never attended his sisters' public appearances, claiming it was embarrassing to see members of his own family perform at recitals and concerts.[13] (Kōko's son, Andō Hiroshi, became a professor specializing in German literature and the music of Richard Wagner at Tokyo University. Under the pen name of Takagi Taku, he was offered the prestigious Akutagawa Award for a historical novel in 1940 but declined to accept it on the ground that the story was inferior to an earlier work of his which had been nominated but failed to receive the same award in 1936.)[14]

Rohan's younger brother, Shigetomo (1873–1954), was the chief editor of *Osaka City Annals*, a longtime professor at Tokyo College of Commerce and Keiō University, and an authority on Japanese economic history and the history of international commerce. His numerous works include a *Kojiki* reader (the entire text annotated and indexed) and the biography of a Confucian scholar and leader of the 1837 famine uprising, *Ōshio Heihachirō*, upon which Mori Ōgai based his novel of the same title. By 1893, Shigetomo also collaborated with Rohan in translating (in part) Leo Tolstoy's *Sevastopol dekabre* from English and *The Great Frozen Sea* by British naval commander Malcolm Hastings. On a government research fellowship, Shigetomo lived in Holland and other European countries from 1928 to 1929.[15] (Rohan himself never indicated an interest in going abroad, despite his love of travel.)

II *Education*

Tsubouchi Shōyō (1859–1935), the scholar-playwright and the mentor of Japanese modern literature, once compared Rohan to Leonardo da Vinci, claiming that Rohan was probably best qualified to represent what could be termed the "Meiji Renaissance" in literature.[16] Like a Renaissance genius, Rohan was a man of many talents, intellectual as well as practical. His nonfiction works include such subjects as mathematical speculation, Neo-Taoist alchemy, theories of urban planning, business practice and ethics, fishing, and even *shōgi* (Japanese chess). A more apt epithet, however, would be *kunshi*, a Confucian scholar-gentleman. His vast knowledge, moral integrity, proud independence, and ceaseless intellectual quest truly earned him the right to be called a great Confucian *kunshi* of Japan. Part of his character was inherited from his parents and nurtured by his family environment, but much was the result of his early education.

From six to nine years of age, Rohan learned reading and writing at a private school. As a child of the samurai class, the seven-year-old Rohan began to attend concurrently another private school where he was taught to recite the texts of Chinese classics, such as the *Book of Filial Piety* (*Hsiao ching*), without much comprehension of its meaning. In this type of recitation known as *sodoku* ("straight reading"), Chinese characters were read in their Japanese pronunciations, adding Japanese particles and auxiliary verbs wherever necessary.[17] One significant effect of *sodoku* is that Chinese classics became a familiar and integral part of the knowledge of Meiji children long before they were old enough to study such works intellectually as foreign philosophy.

In 1875, Rohan entered the elementary school affiliated with Ochanomizu Normal School, the first modern school to experiment with Western educational methods. While other schools were staffed with former *terakoya* ("temple school") teachers, *hankō* ("clan school") instructors, or local intellectuals, this school was taught by student teachers trained at the state-run Ochanomizu Normal School with the curriculum originally established by an American, Marion M. Scott, during the 1872–1874 term of his appointment. Particularly noteworthy is the question-and-answer method employed at this school to stimulate active pupil participation.[18] Rohan finished the eight-year program in four years; and his best subject was arithmetic, presaging his superior aptitude in mathematics and applied sciences which later proved invaluable in his philosophical contemplation of the universe and his study of Neo-Taoism. During this time, he was exposed to *kusazōshi* (Edo period popular storybooks), and Chinese heroic romances such as *All Men Are Brothers* and the *Romance of the Three Kingdoms*, of which he was eventually to publish detailed annotations.

At home, Rohan was taught by his grandmother how to tell time by the stars and how to recognize the various plants in the yard and their medicinal effects.[19] These experiences and habits of observation eventually bore fruit in the form of glossaries such as "Catalogue of Flowers" (1893), "Catalogue of Clouds" (1902), and others. In these works highly regarded by later researchers, Rohan lists names of flowers and clouds, either defining the name ("*Mizumasagumo* mentioned in the Priest Jichin's poem is a name for rain clouds which resemble fish scales, according to a certain book of strategy," XXIX, 224), or invoking poetic imagery ("A red-plum blossom without fragrance is like a woman lacking in poetic sentiment," XXIX, 122). Especially the "Vocabulary of Life on Water" (1897), a dictionary of words concerning life at sea and on rivers ("*Ukigutsu* ['floating shoes'] is a kind of life jacket made of

twenty to thirty small gourds sewn into two long thin bags"
XL, 240) inspired Yanagita Kunio (1875–1962) to launch his
pioneering study of Japanese folklore with his own "Vocabulary
of Fishing Villages" (*Bunrui Gyoson Goi*, completed in 1938).[20]

As a young boy, Rohan tended the family altars and shrines.
It was his daily duty to offer tea and rice to the numerous
household gods and bodhisattvas and keep records of ancestral
anniversaries requiring special offerings. He later recalled:

With all too numerous anniversaries and specific deities' days, my
duties on any given day entailed considerable work. We were
brought up under such strict and rigorous discipline that the work
in itself was not particularly wearisome to me. It was just that not
only did I have to rise terribly early and work swiftly to leave in
time for school, but no one else in the family was allowed to eat
breakfast until I finished making all the offerings properly. Honoring
Buddhas and gods in such a manner had been the generally observed
custom before the Restoration, not at all peculiar to our family.
But because of our conservative grandmother, our family still practiced this custom just as strictly as in our grandfather's days. And I
was the one placed in charge of maintaining it. (XXIX, 204–205)

The significance of such familiarity with Buddhist and Shinto
deities and daily practice of rituals in Rohan's childhood cannot
be overemphasized. Religion was to become an integral part
of Rohan as a man, something with much deeper roots than
mere philosophical speculation or blind faith.

In 1879, Rohan entered the Tokyo First Middle School in
Kanda, founded a year earlier. It is not known exactly what
subjects he studied, except that he excelled in mathematics
again. Only a year later he left this school presumably for
financial reasons, and in 1881 he entered the Tokyo English
School, which boasted a number of foreign teachers. (This
school later merged with a Methodist seminary to become
today's Aoyama Gakuin, well-known for effective teaching of
English.) It was probably due to his family's financial difficulties
that he left this school after one year. During the short time,
however, through his characteristic diligence, he had acquired
serviceable proficiency in English which enabled him later to
read foreign books on science, literature, history, and geography.

His English competence, nevertheless, seems to have been limited to reading comprehension: his daughter, who was educated by foreign missionaries, recalled that Rohan would pronounce the word "lettuce" as *"rettsuse"* (*l* and *r* are phonemically undifferentiated in Japanese); and in his works, Rohan transliterated William as *"uiruriam"* in *kana* syllabary, pronouncing the two *l*'s separately.

In terms of Rohan's character formation and scholarly training, the most significant factors in his life are the Tokyo Library (formerly the Shogunate's Shōheikō Library, and the present National Diet Library) and a private school of Chinese learning called Geigijuku. During 1880–1883, Rohan ravenously read books of all kinds at the library. His almost encyclopedic knowledge in intellectual and practical fields was acquired through his lifetime habit of such avid reading. In the meantime, Rohan began to attend Geigijuku, taught by Kikuchi Shōken (1806–1886), a Confucian scholar of considerable repute. Shōken had taught at Shōheikō, the Shogunate's official Confucian school, where *shushi-gaku* (The Japanese variant of Sung Neo-Confucianism of the Ch'eng-Chu School) was the proclaimed orthodoxy. Shōken naturally emphasized the Confucian canons and history rather than poetry. In addition to lectures, he assigned his students various books of their own choice and conducted discussions in class.

Rohan read widely, thoroughly, and voluminously to satisfy his intellectual curiosity. After he was finished with the Neo-Confucian classics in Shōken's possession, he continued reading at the Library the works of other Confucians and even the "heretical" works such as *Pao-p'u Tzu*, *Lao Tzu*, and *Chuang Tzu* (regarded as the Taoist canon) to the extent that he was sometimes admonished by Shōken. Chizuka Reisui, an author, has recalled the days when he and Rohan were classmates: "Though younger than most of the students at Geigijuku, Rohan was quite mature and usually reticent. Once in class, however, he argued his points squarely, overwhelming his fellow students. Our master, who was a scholar of the Chu Hsi school, taught us to rely on the Chu Hsi commentaries in analyzing the canons. But Rohan often based his views on the older commentaries, stimulating lively discussions in our class."[21] Rohan's natural inclination toward mysticism and such an independent manner of study probably account for the heavy Taoist influence found in his fiction.

Shōken was, moreover, a disciple of Satō Issai (1772–1859),[22] a renowned *shushi-gaku* scholar at Shōheikō who was nonetheless strongly drawn to the teachings of Wang Yang-ming of Ming China. Shōken's library, which was accessible to Rohan, is generally believed to have included many of Wang's writings in addition to *shushi-gaku* texts. Rohan was profoundly influenced by Wang Yang-ming's practical philosophy, especially by his doctrine of the Unity of Knowledge and Action (*chigyō itchi*) based on the belief in innate knowledge (*ryōchi*) as moral intuition and conscience. In 1883, partly prompted by his family's financial difficulty and his father's advocacy of a self-sustaining and productive way of life, Rohan entered a government-run telegrapher's school, which provided students with a monthly stipend as well as free technical education in exchange for three years' service as a telegrapher. He graduated in one year and, after a year's traineeship in Tokyo, was assigned to Yoichi, a town near the present city of Otaru in Hokkaido.

Yoichi was a rather rough but lively boom town abounding in money-making opportunities but not in intellectual activities. Rohan later admitted that he had been "lonely with no friends with whom to exchange knowledge or confide his feeling."[23] He did take with him a trunkful of books, mostly Chinese classics and Buddhist texts, but soon exhausted them. There is an unconfirmed yet quite plausible anecdote which describes Rohan going, in desperation from lack of reading materials, to a nearby temple to borrow all the sutras they had on hand. As a telegrapher, he performed his duties conscientiously. During the fishing seasons, the entire town was bustling day and night, keeping the telegraphers extremely busy. Since most telegrams concerned business dealings, one mistake in a figure could easily cost someone his livelihood. Rohan's later respect for workingmen and his serious view of work may reflect his experiences of this period. Rohan helped the townspeople by offering advice on agriculture, sericulture, hog raising, etc., for which he did research on his own, even sending for books written in English. He also became acquainted with the Ainus. Years later, he was to write a heroic epic story "Snowflakes Dancing" (1889), in which young Ainu chieftains struggle in tragic love and in futile rebellion against bigoted Japanese.

The year 1885, when Rohan was ordered to Hokkaido, has a special significance in Japanese literary history: Tsubouchi Shōyō published *The Essence of the Novel*, in which he introduced and advocated modern realistic literary techniques to supersede the moralistic didactic approach inherited from late Edo literature;[24] and Ozaki Kōyō organized a new literary group, Kenyūsha, which would dominate the Meiji literary scene for the next decade. Sensing an air of literary revival culminating in such events and calling for a lofty type of literature, Rohan became increasingly frustrated at living in remote Hokkaido. At last in August, 1887, he abandoned his post without permission and set out to return to Tokyo.

In a short story called "Dark Side, Bright Side" (1895), he is believed to be summing up his youth to this point in a playful monologue by a fictional old man:

At the age of six or seven, I began to learn how to write . . . , which was the first of my grave mistakes, for as a result, I came to know worthless things. At eight, I was doted on by a girl like a big sister and led to experience jealousy and feelings of inferiority. More regrettably, at thirteen I worshipped such trivial beings as sages and saints and had my soul eroded by didactic teaching, "the Master said that. . . ." At fourteen, my father seemed a fool to me; at fifteen I wanted to imitate the man who was supposed to have lived on grasshoppers and honey; and somehow at sixteen I went mad over heroes, such a pretentious and useless lot. I repented at seventeen and began to release my anguish by means of writing. It is my ill luck that the poison of the writing urge still persists in me. By no means can I expect to come to a good end. . . . I was seized by despicable greed around nineteen. The most perilous was, however, my twenty-first year, known as a crucial age for men. It was indeed the time of life a desperate man must choose between life and death. I barely survived it merely because my soul had been undermined by "the Master said. . . ." Looking back now, I wonder if it might not have been less sinful had I decided then and there, "Should I kill myself? Why not? All right, I will!" (XXIX, 34–35)

In other words, Rohan believed in Confucian teachings; admired John the Baptist; yearned after the heroes of Chinese and Japanese romances; began to write Chinese poetry and philosophical speculations; took a job for a living; and then at the age of twenty-one faced a value crisis in his life.

"A Desperate Journey" (1887), the first of his numerous and well-loved travel journals, describes his trip back to Tokyo from Hokkaido. It begins in a pathetic tone:

Stricken by a malady, my heart was aching. Adverse karma was impossible to dispel; I saw no happy destination in the future but only bitter obstacles before me. I had desires but no money, ambition but no opportunity. At last I decided to break out of this predicament. Selling several kimono and pawning a trunkful of books, I bade farewell to a few friends and departed at once. (XIV, 1)

On horseback, by boat, rickshaw, carriage, and on foot, he reached Kōriyawa in Fukushima Prefecture, intending to take a train for Tokyo:[25]

My feet were aching. Sometimes surrounded by dogs and questioned by people, I finally arrived at Kōriyama at dawn. I had rested many times on the way, at first sitting down on the roadside grass, then throwing my umbrella in the middle of the road to sit on. Finally I lay flat on my back exhausted, with the moonlight flooding my forehead, sadly phantasizing that it might be thus if I were to die on the road some day. (XIV, 1)

His pen name, Rohan the Companion of the Dew, derives from a haiku which is supposed to describe this trip:

Sato tōshi	Far from towns,
Iza tsuyu to nemu	I share with the dew
Kusamakura	A pillow of grass.

This poem appears not in "A Desperate Journey" but in a short story called "Encounter with a Skull" (1890). In the August, 1897, issue of *Shin Shōsetsu*, Rohan explained this origin of his pseudonym.

Back in Tokyo, Rohan found his entire family converted to

Christianity by the influence of Uemura Masahisa, a prominent
Christian theologian as well as an impassioned preacher. Rohan
did not consent to be baptized but attended Uemura's church
services and lectures and read the Bible with the church
members. He took special interest in the Apocalypse, not surprising in view of the unique mystic visions that Rohan later
evoked in his works. Nonetheless, Rohan continued to read
Buddhist sutras and also attended meetings of Buddhism study
groups.

Rohan's youth coincided with a period of Buddhist revival.
On the one hand, Buddhism was trying to survive its post-
Restoration crisis generated by the governmental patronage of
Shintoism at the expense of Buddhist establishments. Buddhist
leaders sought to align Buddhism with the emerging national
consciousness by organizing groups such as Sonnō Hōbutsu
Daidō Dan (Honor the Emperor and Serve the Buddha Union)[26]
to form a common defense with Shintoism against newly imported Christianity. Concurrently, there was a revived interest
in Buddhism among the intellectuals who began to study it
philosophically and metaphysically. Rohan is believed to have
attended meetings of Wakyōkai, a group of such students of
Buddhism.

While helping at a paper store opened by his father, Rohan
read the works of fiction by Ihara Saikaku (1642–1693) and
other writers of the Genroku period (1688–1704) at the suggestion of Awashima Kangetsu (1859–1926), a wealthy dilettante whom Rohan had met at the Tokyo Library.[27] Through
Rohan and Ozaki Kōyō, another friend of Kangetsu's, the re-
discovery of the realistic techniques in the early Edo literature
paved the way toward a literary revival.

III *Rohan the Man*

Rohan is a typically Japanese phenomenon, for he was loved
and worshipped as a person as much as, if not more than, for
his works. The awe and respect for Rohan that can be detected
in writings of other novelists and critics go beyond even the
peculiar conventions of the Japanese literary circle. Even during
his youth, Rohan's name evoked an image of an old philosopher,

erudite and almost awesome. Immediately following his debut into the literary world in his early twenties, he was already referred to as Rohan Oshō (Abbot Rohan) and Rohan Dōjin (Taoist) or Gakujin (Scholar) in the writings of his friends. He himself often signed such pseudonyms to his own works. An author-essayist Masamune Hakuchō (1879–1962) contributed a famous description of Rohan's writing style, saying that it reminded him of an aged samurai walking under the weight of his heavy armor and helmet.[28] Rohan seems to have inspired reverence partly because of an image like a samurai or a monk that became associated with him.

Higuchi Ichiyō (1872–1896), a gifted woman writer who was deeply influenced by Rohan's works, was most anxious to meet him in person. Mori Ōgai's brother brought Rohan to her house on July 20, 1896. Ichiyō's diary records her excitement over the coveted encounter. Her description may be of help in picturing the twenty-nine-year-old Rohan: "He was fair-complexioned, ruddy around the throat, not tall but stoutly built. He spoke serenely in a deep, dignified voice."[29]

Notwithstanding the most memorable photographs of Rohan as a dignified old man with an impressive white beard, he was very much a man of tender feelings, capable of intense passion as revealed in his works, especially the early ones. Well-established in literary circles and having written most of his major works, Rohan married Yamamuro Kimiko in 1896. Tamura Shōgyo, a disciple who lived in Rohan's house for a time, recollected in 1939 that Rohan's wife was "quiet, very considerate of maids and live-in students. She was always modestly dressed yet unquestionably elegant."[30] She managed to save enough money to build a house known as Kagyū-an (Snail's Hut)[31] for Rohan. Kimiko bore him one son and two daughters, kept a happy home while Rohan produced a great volume of work, and died in 1910.[32] In the epitaph on her gravestone, Rohan wrote: "Once she said to me, 'May you long hold to your rocky fortress, for I am well content in poverty.' So selfless and loyal was she."[33] In a touching entry in his diary (July 3, 1910), he relates a dream of a happy fishing trip to the Naruto Channel near Awaji Island.

My wife says, "By the grace of the sacred emperor, you caught this fish. Let's offer our thanks." She holds up the fish still wrapped in the net and bows toward the east. Salt water droplets gleam in the meshes of the net, and the fish scales glisten vermilion in the morning sun. . . . How glorious! I also pray silently in thanksgiving. Presently I raise my head and we look face to face, exchanging smiles. Within a smile bursts an infinite joy. I suddenly feel a poem surging in my heart. Tapping on the gunwale, I recite. . . . My poem seems to overwhelm the roar of the whirlpools.

My own voice awakened me. By my bed was a gloomy lamp; a lonely room. The dawn had not come yet; I felt chilly. I was no longer able to stay in bed. (XXXVIII, 98)

Although Rohan never wrote an autobiographical story, Kimiko nonetheless fills the image of the "ideal wife," whom Rohan defined as a wife who "is concerned with her husband's work as if it were her own, while many a wife loves only her husband but not his work" (XXIX, 113). Their younger daughter and only surviving child, Kōda Aya (1903–), was to become a writer in her own right. After she was separated from her husband, Aya lived with Rohan and cared for him until his death in 1947. At first, she wrote magazine articles concerning Rohan's last days, anecdotes, and memoirs at the request of publishers. Soon, unexpected qualities were noticed in her writings—a uniquely lucid style, poignant wit, penetrating observation, etc.—which brought her unsolicited literary fame, ironically too late for her father to see. As a person, Aya seems a perfect product of Rohan's education based on Chu Hsi's principle of *kakubutsu* ("the investigation of things") and Wang Yang-ming's unity of knowledge and action. After writing *Black Kimono* (1954),[34] which received the Yomiuri Literary Award, she left her only daughter at home and became a maid for a few months in a small geisha house which was fighting off bankruptcy. Based on this experience, she wrote her best novel, *Flowing* (*Nagareru*, 1955).

In his second marriage, however, Rohan was less fortunate. After his elder daughter died of an illness, he realized the futility of trying to raise his children by himself and married Kodama Yayoko in 1912. She was in her forties at the time, born of an influential old family, a devout Christian who studied and taught for a long time in a Christian school. Several poems of Yayoko, under the pen name Kodama Teruko, are included in *Shin Manyōshū* (1937–1938; among the editors were Saitō Mokichi, Kitahara Hakushū, and Yosano Akiko)—eleven volumes of poems of the Meiji, Taisho, and Showa eras. Rohan wrote a preface to this collection.

Rohan's life with Yayoko until her death in 1945 was far from satisfying, beset with constant quarrels over matters extending from discipline of children to religious dogma; her censure of Rohan's drinking; her bitterness after a baby was stillborn; and domestic disorder arising from her inexperience and worsening arthritis.[35] Rohan was driven to ferocious drinking. His daughter describes a scene in which, after a quarrel with his wife, an intoxicated Rohan is working off his anger in the practice of swordsmanship: "With the moon on his back, he was swinging a sword, his white undergarment exposed down to the sash. Flying downward, the white blade glistened and elongated as if to slice the earth. Swung up, it looked short, contracting like a snake. Behind the wall, watching the moonlight and the shadow and the blade and my father, I stood transfixed."[36]

Not only was Yayoko unable to love her husband's work as her own, as expected of an ideal wife, but she refused to accept Rohan's views on life based on Oriental philosophies. Aya relates another revealing anecdote from her childhood:

My stepmother and father were arguing as usual. Father was saying that everything was *kū* ["empty"] and *mu* ["nonexistent"]. She was insisting on the existence of Love. I asked, "What do you mean by *kū* and *mu?*" "They mean that there is nothing," answered father. Unconvinced, I kept asking the same question. He said, "If you think there is something, name it." "There are this kettle and this brazier." "No. They don't exist," he laughed. I pushed his hand against the brazier and said, "See? Your hand is touching it." "But my hand does not exist either." Mystified, I asked, "Does that mean you don't exist either?" "That's right." "That's not true!" Father stared at me and said, "I am not lying. You will see when you have studied more." He walked out of the room, leaving me behind in a weird loneliness. . . . My stepmother then told me that it was a theory of the devil.[37]

Within four years of his second marriage, Rohan wrote fifteen stories (based on episodes in the *Lotus Sutra* and Chinese poems), all of which deal with women's role in love and the beauty of true love, perhaps to abate his own emotional frustrations in marriage.

During World War II, Rohan's diabetes steadily worsened as the material hardships of his daily life increased. The writer Mushakōji Saneatsu (1885–), who met a nearly eighty-year-old Rohan, later recalled: "His eyesight and hearing were growing weak, but blazing vitality was manifest in his speech. He was still an active volcano, by no means extinct."[38] Rohan continued his commentary on Bashō, dictating from his bed. Just as he finished it in 1947, blood from bleeding gums entered his lungs to cause pneumonia, and only a few days after his eightieth birthday, on July 30 (the anniversary of the Emperor Meiji's death), the last of the great Meiji writers was gone. The emperor sent flowers to his funeral, and the mourners included the only socialist premier in Japan's history. Rohan's daughter records his last moments:

Lying on his back, he placed his left hand on his forehead and his right on my bare arm. "Prepared?" he asked. It was a cold hand. I remained silent, not comprehending. He repeated, "Are you prepared?" "Yes, sir, I am prepared," I replied. Part of my father was transplanted in me that moment to forearm me. Without self-deception, I was readied. "Well, then, I shall be gone," he nodded, tapping me with his palm. They were peaceful, expressionless eyes. I felt no particular emotion nor tears. I knew it was the farewell. One word of acknowledgment and the leave-taking was over.[39]

CHAPTER 2

The Idealistic Phase (1889–1893)

I Debut

Ah, the new world of the Meiji era:
How vigorously flourishes its civilization!
But observe the new world of the Meiji era:
How truly appalling is its moral decay!

A man must rise in the world by his virtue;
And a nation must prosper by its moral principles.

. . .

When the spring of prosperity comes to an end,
The warmth of extravagance is no more.
Alas, in the autumn of scattering leaves,
A depraved people fall victim to the Devil,
Their lives ruined and their souls doomed.

Heaven grant I may attain sagehood
And learn the truth!
By word and conduct, I shall propagate it
So mankind may redeem itself.   (XL, 37–38)

WHILE Rohan was a young telegrapher in Hokkaido, he wrote a Chinese poem entitled "A Song of Japan." Beginning with a straightforward adoration, "How beautiful, ah, how beautiful is Japan!," Rohan describes the contemporary cultural scenes blessed with such modern miracles as railroads, telegraph lines, and remarkable medical discoveries. In the second section, however, he cries out, "How tragic, ah, how tragic is Japan!" and deplores that new and decadent ways are prevailing, while laudable traditional customs are vanishing. In the last section (quoted above), he makes a sincere pledge to seek absolute principles and to propagate them through his own practice as

32

well as his literary efforts in order to save mankind from itself. Although the poem may be wanting in stylistic maturity, this youthful, ardent aspiration was never to be forgotten nor to be altered during the remainder of his life. Rohan as a man lived by it and his works, at least for him, never ceased to be an instrument in achieving this goal.

Such fervent love of Japan was by no means unique to Rohan at the time. Around the second decade of the Meiji period, the people's rights movement (*jiyū minken undō*) was sweeping across Japanese society in anticipation of the impending inauguration of the parliamentary system. As people's political consciousness was aroused, there emerged a literary genre called the political novel (*seiji shōsetsu*). The first to become popular was *Inspiring Examples of Eminent Statesmanship (Keikoku Bidan*, 1883-1884) by Yano Ryūkei (1850–1931), a brilliant, versatile man—educator, bureaucrat, and prominent journalist. He was actively involved with the Kaishintō (Progressive Party), most effectively expounding their cause through the newspaper *Yūbin Hōchi*, which he managed as the chief editor. While bedridden with a temporary illness, he read Greek history and was inspired to write this story set in Thebes, focusing on the rebellion of 387 B.C. instigated by despotic Sparta, the restoration of a democratic system by loyal Thebans, and the final victory of Thebes against the powerful Spartan army. Although Ryūkei's primary aim was to enlighten the populace politically, this novel with its fresh characterization, highly charged style, and tense plot greatly inspired the readers.

One year later, in 1885, appeared *Fortuitous Encounters with Beautiful Women (Kajin no Kigū)* by Tōkai Sanshi (1852–1922). Born a samurai's son in Aizu Han, he fought in the Battle of Toba Fushimi in 1868, lost his family in the retaliatory attack by the imperial forces, and was arrested himself. Later he studied economics at Harvard University and at the University of Pennsylvania; and, upon his return, he published this long novel. It proved an instant success, particularly among the educated young men. Borrowing the form of the novel, Tōkai Sanshi expounds his political views through the speeches of his main characters, all exiles from their own countries of lost causes—a daughter of a Spanish constitutionalist general, an Irish lady revolutionary, a Ming Dynasty loyalist, and the student protagonist (whose name became the author's pen name, meaning a stroller of the Eastern sea) from the Aizu Han, the last holdout and the most courageous pro-Tokugawa force on the eve of the Meiji Restoration. In this book, the author describes the histories of nations with lost causes and warns of the similar crisis imminent within contemporary Japan. Tōkai Sanshi's impassioned patriotism cast him as a champion of *Nihonshugi* (Japanism)—idealistic love of Japan with a new international awareness—which extolled the beauty of things Japanese and advocated the need for Japan to establish itself in the world as a modern nation.

The Meiji twenties (1887–1896), when Rohan made his literary debut, was a paradoxical period in Japanese cultural history. Westernization was encouraged and promoted by the government, in an effort to present a more modern image of Japan so as to facilitate favorable treaty revisions with foreign nations. But at the same time, in preparation for the 1889 promulgation of the constitution and in support of its subsequent enforcement, the government was carefully cultivating a nationalism reinforced by the absolute monarchy and a revival of Confucian ethics, both distinctly nonmodern policies. An official expression of such state policy was to appear as the Imperial Rescript on Education of 1890, prescribing the virtues of loyalty to the Emperor, patriotism, and filial piety. Such governmental moves induced a number of reactions. One was *heiminshugi* ("democratism") advocated by Tokutomi Sohō (1863–1957) and the magazine *Kokumin no Tomo* (1887–1897), calling for more democratic (people-initiated), spontaneous Westernization. Another was *kokusuishugi* ("national essence-ism") led by Miyake Setsurei (1860–1945) and other editors of the magazine *Nihonjin* (1888–1907). The latter were anti-Westernization nationalists advocating national independence and integrity, based on aesthetic love of Japan for its natural beauty and traditional culture.

Rohan read, while in Hokkaido, at least the first three volumes of *Fortuitous Encounters with Beautiful Women* published between October, 1885, and February, 1887. Rohan's own "Song of Japan" is inspired by this book, particularly by "At the

Independence Hall," a Chinese poem composed by the protagonist in Philadelphia. More literary than political in his temperament, however, Rohan was never inclined to be a fanatic ideologist. His patriotic fervor prompted him instead to become a writer with only one ambition—to help make the new Japan better.

Rohan's first printed work is an essay entitled "Sound and Words," which appeared in the January, 1887, issue of a magazine called *Kunshi to Shukujo* (*Gentlemen and Ladies*). In a discussion of traditional Japanese music and the newly imported Western music, he appeals to the readers to help raise the status of the Japanese composer at least to the level of the lyricist so that they can together develop new music befitting the Meiji period. His first short story, however, was not fortunate enough to survive. Sometime around 1888, he wrote "Secular Zen, the Arch Demon" in the manner of the late Edo popular literature, about a man who engages in Zen meditation in a courtesan's chamber. This work is not extant, for Rohan is said to have used the manuscript to repair sliding paper doors. Fortunately, he had shown the work to Kangetsu, who in turn handed it to Kōyō, the chief editor of *Garakuta Bunko*. Kōyō was sufficiently impressed and asked Rohan to write a new story specifically for his magazine. "One Instant," which appeared in *Bunko*[1] in July, 1889, was written for Kōyō.

Rohan's first published work of fiction, however, was a longer and more ambitious story which came out earlier in February in an influential fiction magazine called *Miyako no Hana*. Its managing editor Yamada Bimyō (1868–1910) was then overshadowing Kōyō with his emotional romanticism and the fresh *genbun itchi* ("unity of spoken and written languages") style.[2] It was Kangetsu who arranged for Rohan's debut work, "Dewdrops," to be published. He introduced Rohan to Yoda Gakkai (1833–1903), who was influential at the time as a writer and critic. Gakkai's diary records that Rohan brought the story to him, saying, "I have written this work to embody a certain ideal. If it measures up to your standards, please write a preface for me."[3] "Dewdrops" was immediately published with a glowing preface by Gakkai.

The story begins as Bunseimu (an American in New York

City), an unschooled yet wise self-made man of vast wealth, places a want ad in the newspapers seeking a suitable husband for his beautiful and intelligent daughter, Rubina. There is only one major qualification—that it be a man who can lead a cheerful life without ever finding anything unpleasant. A young Unitarian minister, Shinzia, is in love with Rubina but, being a man of principles, he refuses to apply for the qualifying tests. Among numerous applicants, only a Japanese poet substituting for his wealthy Chinese patron is about to be pronounced the winner because he has shown no displeasure at various exasperating, insulting tests. (For example, he is naturally impervious to derogatory remarks heaped upon him which would have provoked a real Chinese.) A man by nature footloose and fancy-free as well as a mere proxy in fear of disclosure, the poet flees in the night. Bunseimu gives Rubina's hand to Shinzia, who demonstrated true sincerity by declining to prove his love by tests; and Bunseimu invites the Japanese poet back as his carefree companion to accompany him on a poetic trip around the world.

"Dewdrops" is unlike any of Rohan's subsequent works in many respects. Rohan seems quite at ease in using the *genbun itchi* style for dialogue and the literary style for the narrative portion. The imagery is obviously Western: Rubina is called the White Rose of Dawn, and Shinzia is described as "gentle as sheep in the heavenly garden." Names are juxtapositions of English and Japanese: Shinzia is a Japanization of "sincere," while Bunseimu is an Americanization of (Kinokuniya) Bunzaemon, a heroic adventurer of legendary fame who made a fortune in tangerines and the shipping business during the seventeenth century. The scene is set in contemporary New York and China, but it is an idealized America envisioned and aspired to by the Japanese of the early Meiji. The characters, all Americans and Chinese except for one Japanese, do not yet exhibit typically Rohanesque forceful individualities.

Yet sincerity, which was to become the core of Rohan's "ideal," already plays an important, even central, role here in close connection with the plot development. The subplots involving the tests and a substitute suitor were transposed from a Chinese popular story, "Master Ch'ien Wins Miss Feng Unexpectedly," included in *Chin-ku-ch'i-kuan*, a collection of Ming period tales. The difference between the Chinese story and "Dewdrops" is most revealing. The Chinese father of the intended bride was a wealthy money lender seeking a son-in-law superior in looks as well as in scholarly aptitude, which in China of the day directly related to social and financial success. The protagonist was accepted even after he was discovered to be a substitute for his rich but unattractive cousin, solely because of his handsome appearance and his reputation as an excellent student. The Chinese story offered neither love theme nor emphasis on personal integrity, and did not contain the concept of *fūryū* (poetic enjoyment of nature and emotional freedom) as submerging of the self into the universe.

Such a nebulous relationship between Rohan's works and their sources was to become a pattern throughout his career. It is generally quite difficult to pinpoint sources of influence on Rohan, because any similarities found between his stories and possible sources are usually indecisive and partial. In his own preface to "Dewdrops," however, Rohan acknowledges that "despite its plot reminiscent of Lytton and Thackeray,[4] this story has a source that must be obvious to learned readers" (VII, 3).

The themes which were eventually to blossom in his later and more representative works are already suggested in "Dewdrops." The love between Rubina and Shinzia is not only descriptive of the new and ideal mode of love conceived in the mind of early Meiji youth, but it also heralds Rohan's theory of love, which embraces an innocent, spiritual, and fairy-talelike aspect. And the concept of *fūryū*, as practiced by the carefree Japanese poet and the worldly-wise, openhearted Bunseimu, was later developed into a very complex view of art, man, and nature. "Dewdrops" may at first glance appear to echo the exoticism and Westernization craze prevalent in that period, but more careful reading will reveal Rohan's critical attitude toward such contemporary taste. While the typical ambition of early Meiji youth was focused on social success, Rohan presents Bunseimu, who has already achieved social and financial success, through the masculine and vigorous whaling business, rather than though sycophancy and unabashed duplicity, such as demonstrated by Honda Noboru in *Ukigumo* (*Drifting Clouds*, 1887–1889) by Futabatei Shimei (1864–1909). Rohan's American setting is an inevitable choice: it is a society where the dominant concern is presumably no longer focused on social success itself but rather on how to enjoy its fruit without losing human values; moreover, it is a society with a seemingly solid moral basis provided by Christianity.

The influence of Christian humanism also accounts for Rohan's emphasis on human life and enjoyment of life here and now. Since a Christian is to be judged solely by his actions in this life, his salvation rests entirely on how he lives in this world. A Christian cannot afford to compromise with evil, for he will have no other life to undo his wrongs as can Buddhists, whose souls are supposed to transmigrate through innumerable lives. Hence the importance of sincerity, steadfast adherence to principles, as stressed in "Dewdrops." Unitarianism, which figures large in this story, was first introduced to Japan by Yano Ryūkei in a series of articles appearing in the *Yūbin Hōchi* from 1886 to 1887. The Unitarian view of Christ as a religious hero seems to affirm human attainment of moral perfection rather than Christ's divine origin; and no less significant is the Unitarian emphasis on future happiness instead of past sins. Rohan's novels have few tragic endings, for his characters achieve happiness in some form or find a ray of hope in some way at the end of their painful struggle. Since Rohan's concept of happiness is in the state of mind, money and position are irrelevant to happiness, just as Bunseimu believed in "Dewdrops." Hence a man is honored only for himself and for his way of life.

It was with this idealistic story that Rohan launched into a career through which he intended to define the moral order of the universe. Thanks to its novel plot, exotic setting, expansive vision, accomplished *gazoku setchū bun* (a mixture of poetic and colloquial styles), and unique theme, "Dewdrops" was received with enormous enthusiasm. According to the report of the literary essayist-critic Uchida Roan (1868–1929), the editor Yamada Bimyō exclaimed: "What a genius! What an exciting story! You can never tell when and where a genius might emerge, just like a comet."[5]

II "*Love Bodhisattva*"

Rohan's place in the literary world was firmly established with his next work, "Love Bodhisattva." It appeared in September, 1889, in the fifth issue of the *Shincho Hyakushu* (*A Hundred New Stories*) series, which had earlier carried Kōyō's first widely acclaimed story, "Confessions of Love Affairs" (*Irozange*, February, 1889). "Love Bodhisattva" tells of a Buddhist sculptor called Shu'un who sets out on a journey in quest of artistic perfection. He comes upon a house where Tatsu, vendor of preserved flowers, is held prisoner by her violent uncle who is planning to sell her to a brothel. When Shu'un brings her back to his inn, the kindly innkeeper takes it upon himself to arrange matrimony between Shu'un and the grateful Tatsu. With no intention of accepting such repayment for his gallant action, Shu'un steals out of the inn, only to fall ill in another town. Tatsu comes to nurse him back to health, and he finally falls in love with her. On the night of their wedding, however, Tatsu is forced to leave Shu'un by a messenger from her long lost samurai father, now a viscount.

Brokenhearted, Shu'un carves an image of Tatsu, at first clad in kimono. In an attempt to recapture the true beauty of Tatsu as she appeared in his dreams, he shaves off all the garments and ornaments from the wooden image. In the end emerges a divinely beautiful nude statue of a bodhisattva. When he reads a newspaper article announcing Tatsu's impending marriage to a young nobleman, he tries in anger to destroy the almost lifelike statue. Finding himself unable to touch his own work, he breaks down in tears. Suddenly the statue appears to move.

Did they descend from heaven or spring out of the earth? Smooth arms warmly wrapped around his neck and soft hair fragrantly caressed his cheeks. Quickly turning, he found Tatsu just as he remembered her. "Is it you, Tatsu?" Shu'un embraced and kissed her on the forehead. Did the statue come to life? Did the girl return? Unwise to ask, too long to explain. (I, 76–77)

In the last chapter, Shu'un and Tatsu ascend to heaven man and wife, followed by believers in Tatsu the bodhisattva, including even her evil uncle.

The synopsis may read like a melodrama, but the impact of "Love Bodhisattva" was immense. In the February, 1890, issue of *Kokumin no Tomo*, a prestigious intellectual magazine, appeared a review entitled "Last Year's Masterpieces" by Ishibashi Ningetsu (1865–1926)—a rising critic of the day. He cited "Love Bodhisattva" as the most prominent work of the year and praised its "carefully selected subject matter, marvelously conceived ideas, and pervading verve." And Ningetsu expressed hope that Rohan would continue on to reach the pinnacle of excellence and become Japan's Goethe, with visions of higher realms. More emotional reactions included the memoirs of Tayama Katai (1871–1930), the pioneer of Japanese naturalism (*shizenshugi*): "With the appearance of 'Love Bodhisattva' and the 'Confessions of Love Affairs' [by Kōyō], my heart and soul burned with yearning for a new Japanese literature."[6]

Even Masaoka Shiki (1867–1902), who later revitalized Japanese traditional poetry by means of realistic techniques, acknowledged the initial effect of "Love Bodhisattva" on his own artistic ambition:

The plot of "Love Bodhisattva" is basically borrowed from the West and rearranged into a Japanese setting. It boldly deals with a nude beauty, quite a controversial subject even today. Instead of finding it the least bit lewd, however, I felt myself lifted toward heaven in a sublime air. I used to regard the *Character Sketches of Contemporary Students* [1885–1886, by Tsubouchi Shōyō] as the only worthy model of the genre, but my opinion reversed itself at this point. I began to believe that "Love Bodhisattva" was the loftiest of novels and that if one were to write a novel at all, one must emulate Rohan. . . . For some time afterward, I was almost delirious with a feverish wish to author even one novel like it in my lifetime. I, who had neglected fiction writing until then, almost longed to turn myself into a character in a novel to act out such emotions.[7]

In 1893, Shiki did compose a romantic story entitled "The Moon Capital" (*Tsuki no Miyako*) and asked for Rohan's critical opinion. Discouraged by an unfavorable response, Shiki decided to concentrate his creative talent on haiku, and the rest is literary history.

"Love Bodhisattva" caused a sensation for two reasons: one

was its striking style, the other, its intensely poetic imagination. After its culmination in *Ukigumo*, the *genbun itchi* movement was beginning to show signs of stagnation, and newly discovered Saikaku and Genroku literature were sparking great interest in realistic techniques and classical Japanese style. "Love Bodhisattva" was Rohan's answer to the stylistic confusion of the time. His feelings toward the *genbun itchi* style are revealed in an article discussing Kōyō's "A Woodsman's Love" (*Koiyamagatsu*, 1889). Rohan attributes the richness of Kōyō's style to his refusal to resort to "the so-called Russian style grammar similar to a cross section of a geological chart" (XXIV, 29). Elsewhere, he also denounces the attempt to unify spoken and written languages as based on a fallacy that the purpose of written language is to copy speech, as if speech were the child of thought, and writing its grandchild. He points out that speech at any given historical time is in the process of constant evolution and therefore cannot be accorded the leading position over writing. And especially in the case of Japanese, which is not a speech-oriented language, a writer must aspire to succeed in transcribing thought directly and faithfully into writing (XXV, 53–57). Rohan's "On Illusiveness of Sound" (1944) is an attempt to grasp the transitional processes of spoken Japanese.

In "Love Bodhisattva," Rohan successfully employs two vastly different styles: a facile, vernacular, humorous, fluent style for the first eight sections; and after Shu'un begins to carve the image, a terse, rhythmic, intense style. The latter, which is better-known as typically Rohanesque, is reminiscent of Saikaku's style, with effective omission of particles, suggestively strong sentence endings with nouns instead of verbs, and juxtaposition of long and short cadences. Even more significantly, Rohan creates startling shifts in mood by the use of either heavily Chinese word clusters or soft Japanese constructions.

In the scene where the wooden image seems to change into a living girl, a sentence quoted earlier reads in Japanese: "tama no kaina wa atatakaku waga kubisuji ni karamarite, kumo no bin no ke nioyaka ni hoho o naderu o ..." ("Smooth arms warmly wrapped around his neck, and soft hair fragrantly caressed his cheeks ..."). Such predominantly feminine and sensory imagery comes as a relief, for it is preceded by an extremely heavy and abstract style describing Shu'un just as he completes the statue: "Koko ni kesō no hanagoromo, gen'ei kūge gedatsu shite, jinnyū musai jōju issai, sōgon tanrei arigataki jissō mimyō no fūryū-butsu" ("The flowery robe of temporary truth was sublimated like an illusion of ethereal blossoms achieving the profound, boundless consummation; here, the love bodhisattva, an ex-quisite reality in incomparable majesty and grace") (I, 66).

The mellifluous first passage has eight nouns (five of which designate parts of the human body), two adjectives, two verbs, and as many as eight particles. The second passage is composed of fifteen nouns (all of which are abstract or symbolic), a single adjective, and a lone verb in the middle, with only four particles in all. The latter is, moreover, conspicuous because of the re-peated occurrence of the harsh g and j sounds, double con-sonants, and long vowels. Its basic seven and five syllable rhythm, Chinese style parallel construction, and noun endings might otherwise make it static and pedestrian, but the heavy use of Buddhist words leaden with abstract concepts and abrasive sounds helps slow down the passage and adds depth to the scene, evoking the chiseling rhythm and a mystic vision.[8] The flexible and dynamic style of "Love Bodhisattva" contributed immensely to the flourishing of *gazoku setchū* style in its time.

In this tale, Rohan pursues the theme of love and sincerity to an artistic and mystic crystallization. Despite its first im-pression of classicism, this story deals with a new view of love, unexpectedly rendered in classical guise. The setting is con-temporary Meiji society, where a traditional horror of love as delusion (as preached to Shu'un by the innkeeper) was still deep, concurrent with a Western-inspired awareness that one must be true to one's own emotions. Shu'un sets out in search of national pride so that Japanese artists need no longer suffer the contempt of "Westerners with long noses like plaster statues." In the end, however, it is not Westernization itself that is negated. After all superficialities are stripped off, the wooden statue emerges as modern and Western as a marble sculpture—love in its humanizing and redeeming essence; and Tatsu the bodhisattva is said to manifest herself in a long velvet gown and a tiara with ostrich plumes as often as in shabby kimono and straw sandals, testifying to the universality of love and art that transcends ethnic boundaries.

CHAPTER 3

Emergence of the Rohanesque Hero and Heroine

I Early Works

THUS began the first phase of Rohan's writing career. During 1889, Rohan wrote four more stories. "Surprise!" is a short mystery about an attempted jewel swindle by two Europeans ending in the victory of a smart Japanese pawnbroker aided by his nephew (a new bachelor of science). "How Suspicious!" concerns an evil Count Shylock who violates beautiful Quickly and poisons her father. While the gravely ill father is taking mercurous chloride medicine for his fever, the count makes him ingest dilute hydrochloric acid. When the father dies, the count drinks the same fluid to prove it harmless before witnesses. Upon learning that this particular chemical combination produces a deadly poison, mercuric chloride, Police Chief Bright employs a number of people to impersonate ghosts, and uses a slide projector to frighten the count with the images of drowned Quickly and her blood-spouting father, while dimming the lamp by secretly mixing water into the oil. Bright has an actor play a saintly hermit who advises the count to absolve himself of all sins by writing a confession in order to be cured of mental affliction. Throughout his career, Rohan showed an affinity for detective stories and mysteries in which he utilized his knowledge of pure and applied sciences, psychology, and psychic phenomena—for example, a secret message written in invisible ink in "Dewdrops," and a clever murder by arsenic used in sericulture in "Blank-eyed Daruma" (1897). Rohan's knowledge of sciences and psychology proved valuable in his lifelong study of Neo-Taoist alchemy and Taoist philosophy.

The next was "A Rare Man," the first of his samurai tales.

Murakami Kiken (Willing Sword), a muscular samurai over six feet tall, is mortified by the decline of the samurai spirit, when Lord Asano's death goes unavenged by his retainers. Kiken leaves the service of his own lord in Kyushu and journeys northeast toward Akō, Lord Asano's domain, carrying a superb sword on whose sheath is written, "Willing to die any time." He finally catches Ōishi Kuranosuke, the highest-ranking Asano vassal, at a drunken party in the gay quarters and kicks him like a dog. Before long, Kiken learns of the successful revenge carried out in 1702 by the famed forty-seven loyal retainers led by Ōishi after months of careful preparation. One night, Kiken commits ritual disembowelment before Ōishi's tomb in Sengaku Temple, where even today a lone grave marker stands bearing the name "Kiken." Short and simple in plot as this story is, Kiken is a forerunner of Rohanesque heroes with an idealistic determination, scornful of compromise. Rohan's later heroes are to develop more depth and facets to their character through bitter trials and painful labor on their way to the final goal.

The last story in 1889 was "Snowflakes Dancing" in thirteen installments amounting to thirty-five pages. It was discontinued due to changes in editorial policies of the *Yomiuri* after this newspaper was suspended for a brief period by government censorship. The story was originally conceived to be a grand-scale heroic epic based in part on the actual Ainu rebellion of the 1660s. Rohan finished up to the point where the hero Shagushain is about to marry Irabu, a sister of his friend, Chief Onbishi, while a corrupt Japanese official in charge of Ainu affairs is anxious to make her his mistress. Ten years later, in consultation with Rohan, a disciple finished the story based on Rohan's original plan. It seems that Rohan had conceived the plot of this story already in his Hokkaido days, for a poem in "Dewdrops" (supposedly composed by one of the suitors in response to a riddle) unfolds a similar story in which immediately after a wedding, the enemies (the Japanese) attack across the border and the husband is killed; the wife subsequently weeps herself literally blind, wanders into the mountains, and finally freezes to death on Shakotan Peak. The story as it stands now rather faithfully follows this plot and is a touching romance, though lacking Rohan's own forceful style.

"Snowflakes Dancing" was to be a tragedy, rare among Rohan's works, and also the first of his semihistorical novels. In the preface, Rohan discloses that only the personalities are borrowed from the actual incident. Shagushain, who massacred over two hundred and seventy Japanese in the last of the Ainu rebellions, is described as a tall, masculine, heavily bearded, and clear-eyed youth in his twenties: the real Shagushain was believed to have been an old man by the time of the uprising. Onbishi, the other leader, was actually a man of wisdom who refused to join Shagushain in the futile rebellion which he considered detrimental to the welfare of the Ainus. In "Snowflakes Dancing," however, Onbishi is a close friend and brother-in-law of Shagushain, eventually to fight side by side for the same cause. Rohan later denounced this novel for being like a "colorless flower that only shows an outline without conveying emotion" (VII, 155). Even though Shagushain is undeniably cast as a Rohanesque hero of vision and stature, Rohan later turned away from this approach to historical novels: in his unique historical biographies beginning with "Yoritomo" (1908), he followed historical records faithfully and at the same time achieved emotional impact, quiet yet long-lasting.

In December, 1889, Rohan was invited to join the *Yomiuri* literary section headed by Tsubouchi Shōyō. Ozaki Kōyō became a regular staff writer at this time, but Rohan asked for an associate status on half pay, probably to secure more free time for his own literary activities and studies. In 1890, Rohan wrote for the *Yomiuri* seven short minor satires ridiculing man's hypocrisy and vanity, and five installments of "A Bearded Man," a story about a samurai who believes that true loyalty lies in trying to live as long as possible in order to accomplish a worthy deed rather than in following the lord in death after a decisive defeat. This story was terminated due to a change in plot as well as Rohan's illness. (A revised version was completed in 1896.)

II *"Encounter With a Skull"*

More ambitious works appeared in literary magazines during 1890: "Encounter With a Skull," embodying one of the twin pinnacles in Rohan's view of life and salvation; "Venomous Coral Lips," considered to be a prelude to "Encounter With a Skull"; and "A Sword," the first of his artisan stories.

"Encounter With a Skull" is a tale of mystical beauty and haunting visions. A brash young man called (Young) Rohan loses his way in the mountains beyond Nikko. He stumbles into a lonely hut and spends a disquieting night with an unearthly beauty, who unnerves him with an invitation to share the only bed in the house. He manages to stay up by asking her to tell the story of her life. The woman, Tae, had been a wealthy, happy girl until her mother died, leaving a letter which condemned her to a celibate life. A young nobleman fell hopelessly in love with her and finally died of a broken heart. One day Tae in feverish madness followed the young man's phantom into the mountains, where a saintly hermit taught her to accept all things with good grace. Young Rohan asks what was written in her mother's letter which so drastically altered her life; her only reply is that it revealed the accursed fate of her family. With the first sign of sunlight, the house and the woman vanish, leaving Young Rohan in a desolate field with a bleached white skull at his feet. Upon reaching a village, Young Rohan learns from an innkeeper that a mad leper woman disappeared into the mountains some time earlier in the year.

There is little wonder that "Encounter With a Skull" should have earned Rohan many admirers. (The most enthusiastic of them was Tanizaki Jun'ichirō, who wrote similar stories of eerie visions.) Its structure is reminiscent of *Nō* plays, in which the protagonist undergoes metamorphosis, usually from a humble disguise to the spirit of a dead nobleman suffering because he is still undelivered from his former self, revealing the pathos of this world and visions of the life after death. Rather than an aged traveling monk as in most *Nō* plays, it is a still immature young man who encounters the heroine in this story. The metamorphosis of the charming hostess of the night is more complex and philosophical than the typical *Nō* version. A beauty changes into an abomination in reality, and a grotesque skull projects an image of a perfect, ideal woman transcending the limitations imposed by the flesh. Even beyond simple relativism or contrast, Rohan penetrates into human existence not only to delineate it but to pursue its ultimate meaning. Young Rohan's travel through the mountains is at once a journey within his psyche, a classic voyage (ascending in this case) into the realm of the subconscious, where, Rohan believed, all distinctions such as good and evil would be meaningless. Young Rohan comments: "While my body was damp with perspiration from the ordeal of climbing, I felt as if the defiling robes of the Five Desires clouding my mind had begun to peel off one by one. The Devil of Consciousness, who had raged unchecked in all his supernatural glory until the day before, now appeared humbled, having been deprived of his allies and kin. Somehow I lost my nerve; I felt as if I were a fugitive fleeing from the entire world" (I, 139).

When the woman asks him to sleep in the same bed, the horrified Young Rohan recites frantically the "Elimination of Desires," a Chinese poem warning against lust. Then in his mind he continues a seriocomic monologue describing an imaginary scene:

For me to keep calm would be difficult indeed under such circumstances. It would be nearly impossible with her downy locks brushing against my cheeks and her radiant face right in front of my nose. Where would she put her soft arms? Where could her breasts hide? This surely is a serious situation. How could I possibly fall asleep as calmly as if holding a female cat in my arms? Oh, no! Suppose our clothes became undone through casual movements of our bodies, unseen under the cover? And what if her shapely legs or feet touched my own hairy shins? Good heavens! That would be a moment of life and death for me! Being a mediocre man, basically quite shaky in willpower and always remiss in observing the moral commandments, at best I would lose a peaceful night's sleep; that is, if I were able to control my baser instincts. (I, 149–50)

Such sensuous images, even though in a chimerical bed scene, add to the terrifying implication innate in the temptation of the flesh, for at the end the same woman is identified as having been a disfigured leper in a quite unique and graphic description of physical deterioration:

Her face was even more horrible, looking like a half-melted copper lion. With all the eyebrows gone, the prominent forehead was marred by deep hollows filthier than faded purple rubbed with ditch mud, oozing yellowish grey pus like rotten oysters pouring out of the shells. . . . The festered lip exposed sparse yellow teeth and thin pale gums in a cruel contrast; out of the cheek split toward the right glared the molars. Her hairless head glistened weirdly as shiny as a well-rubbed red gourd. . . . The underlid of the bulging left eye was turned inside out so that the red veins were clearly visible, the white of the eye clouded in greyish-yellow. The glazed brown pupil was almost immobile, glowering up at man, gods, and Buddhas. From time to time she would take a deep sigh as if disgorging a bodyful of virulent air, and even dogs and birds fled from her. (I, 165–66)

Such contemplation of gothic horrors may remind Western readers of Baudelaire. There is, however, no indication that Rohan had read Baudelaire before the composition of "Encounter With a Skull." Rohan is not known to have had even a reading knowledge of French; Baudelaire's *Les Fleurs du Mal* was not introduced to Japan until it was first mentioned by Mori Ōgai in 1892 and discussed by Ueda Bin (1874–1916, a translator) in 1900.[1] Rohan's description of leprosy is in the tradition of such medieval picture scrolls as "Disease Scroll" (*Yamai-zōshi*) and "Hell Scroll" (*Jigoku zōshi*).

"Encounter With a Skull" offers yet another aspect to be considered. Both the beautiful maiden and the repulsive mad leper represent the past phases of the spirit who speaks through a mysterious woman projected into Young Rohan's mind by the skull. She is in fact a divine being, neither a man nor a woman, for she can calmly accept and embrace all things and beings as "a wet nurse holds a child in love" without passing judgment. Her realm of perfect contentment affirms one way of achieving salvation: submerging the self totally into the universe until one is identified with all souls. Young Rohan notes: "If I feel compassion for another, he will love me in turn. If we mutually sympathize and love, I am within him, and he within me. Since there is no distance between us, we perceive each other's emotions and thoughts, and our boundaries tally. A skull in a secluded valley attracted the mind of a lone traveler in the present time, and a lonely traveler in the deep mountain perceived the former life of the skull" (I, 164–65).

(This story was translated by Miyamori Asatorō in 1914 as "Lodging for the Night" in *Representative Tales of Japan*. For some inexplicable reason, Miyamori omitted the last section quoted above, unjustifiably altering the intent and effect of the story.)

At any rate, Tae is most typical of the Rohanesque heroine with feminine beauty and masculine spirit. Quite consistent with the egalitarian mood of the early Meiji, Rohan's heroines are endowed with self-identity and capable of fighting their battles to determine their own fate, reflecting also the way Rohan's talented sisters made life meaningful for themselves.

In a comic satire, "Venomous Coral Lips," a handsome and high-spirited woman living alone in a mountain hermitage confesses to a young suitor that she is in love with the Buddha, who wrote the most beautiful love poems in the world known as sutras. By a romantic acceptance of human emotions, this woman humanizes a religious concept (the Buddha) into a poet who was moved by his emotion (pity for the suffering people) to preach the way of salvation. This minor tale is generally considered to show the process through which Tae in "Encounter With a Skull" achieved her enlightenment.

III *The Concept of Love*

Rohan's works as a whole reflect three views on love, not mutually exclusive. The first concerns love on the physical level. From a Buddhist point of view, woman is an object of lust— unclean, basically sinful; and she is the cause of evil, for lustful desire is a powerful obstacle in achieving enlightenment. The lust chapter (*Aiyoku-bon*) of the *Hokku-gyō* (*Dhamma-pada Sutra*) teaches that lust is the cause of anguish and fear. Tae with her supposedly hereditary leprosy is a personification of lust that defiles and destroys all who are ensnared by her surface beauty. Young Rohan already knows that love is the cause of suffering, if instinctively, for he recites a Chinese poem, "Elimination of Desires," to protect himself against the harm of love.

Physical love per se is completely negated in "Encounter With a Skull": Tae is absolutely forbidden love by her mother

and by karma; and a young nobleman's ardent love is destined
to destroy him and drive Tae on a frenzied journey. The little
hut in the mountain represents the physical world, which is
merely an illusion (a dream) induced by a skull and in which
sexual love means an evil karma, basically injurious and even
deadly. That is why Tae protects Young Rohan by dressing
him in a woman's kimono and regarding him as a wet nurse
would a child. Only when a man realizes the true emptiness
and pathos of physical love, can he attain a universal relationship with all things and all beings. So when a woman no
longer seems unclean, that is, when a woman is no longer a
woman but simply a human being, love's evil hold is broken
and the oneness of all beings revealed.

On the other hand, neither Buddhism nor Rohan altogether
repudiate heterosexual love as such: love can be a means to
a union of two souls, for true love between man and woman
demands total abandonment of one's self into the other. As the
character for Confucian humanity *jen* consists of man plus
the numeral two, moreover, love between two persons can extend
to universal love. In his "Iśāna's Garden" (1915), Rohan refers
to an episode from the *Kegon Sutra*. Zenzai-dōji in quest of
knowledge comes to Iśāna, wife of a king, and learns of one
means to achieve salvation called *dōrui gyōmon* (group practice
of the "Law"). Rohan explains it as a type of universal love
but points out its uniqueness in the emphatic insistence that
salvation be achieved collectively only with the same kind
(*dōrui*), that is, those who gather in Iśāna's beautiful garden
with the same desire to attain salvation. Such a belief is more
human and feminine, comments Rohan, than the egalitarian
bodhisattva concept presupposing the possibility of universal
salvation; but love between lovers can also be considered the
first level of *dōrui gyōmon* where the man and the woman
may represent all men and women. Love, moreover, serves to
create equality among all people, Rohan suggests, for it renders
a man eager to submit to the weaker sex, and it teaches both
man and woman to be truly humane.

The second view of love is similar to Christian romanticism,
which sees the image of God in Christ, a human, who was
the proof of God's love for mankind. On this level, love is no

longer simply a human emotion but an all-embracing, extra-
mundane grace, and aspiration toward the infinite, and the
affirmation of the absolute. The statue-turned-bodhisattva is a
personification of love, not only human love but also divine
love, for it has the power to enlighten mankind. Love, then,
is in itself sacrosanct and precious to Rohan. Love becomes a
universal and fundamental human feeling, when passion and
poetic imagination are liberated from reason and conventional
ethics. It is in this spirit that Tae offers to embrace Young
Rohan, and the woman in "Venomous Coral Lips" loves the
Buddha. A romantic view of woman as a spiritual symbol and
a guide to salvation had already been immortalized in the
Divine Comedy and Goethe's *Faust*, but within Japanese tradition Rohan's view reflects the image of women in such *Nō*
plays as *Dōjōji* (*Dōjō Temple*) and *Yamauba* (*The old lady
of the mountain*).

The *yamauba* reveals her multiple identity as a companion
in love (courtesan), a female demon (Hannya), and also as a
guiding spirit who has attained the knowledge that good and
evil are one and all things are the same. She is found in places
where the tall peaks symbolize *jōgubodai* (aspiration toward
Buddhahood) and deep valleys signify *gekeshujō* (enlightenment of mankind), but she has no permanent dwelling of her
own. Rohan's annotation (in 1916) of this *Nō* play states: "I
think that the above passage implies her immanent presence
throughout the universe" (XL, 399). Tae and Tatsu are the
eternal and ever-present woman symbolized by the *yamauba*,
who can cause man's downfall, suffers from her own nature,
and attains a sacred status. The *yamauba* is also identified
with the female demon called Hannya. The word *hannya* as
used in *Hannya-gyō* (*Prajñāpāramitā Sutras*) is a translation
of *prajñā*, the ultimate knowledge in Buddhist terms. The
yamauba herself declares that traveling from mountain to
mountain (pilgrimage) and helping tired woodcutters and
weavers (the bodhisattva practice), she has transformed herself
into a nonhuman by the power of her faith. Rohan comments:
"With such faith, she could not possibly fail to attain Buddhahood" (XL, 400).

As for woman's attainment of Buddhahood, Mahayana sutras

(except the *Lotus Sutra*) either disregard this problem or deny the possibility altogether. (In the Hinayana or *Theravada* sutras, there are some suggestions of Buddha's accepting the possibility of woman's attaining Buddhahood, but here we are concerned only with the Mahayana tradition, which was formative for Rohan and Japanese Buddhism as a whole.) One reason for denying woman's Buddhahood is the belief that its attainment requires a brave and indomitable spirit, presumably lacking in the inherently sentimental woman. Nevertheless, what poses the insurmountable problem is another reason: the Buddha is supposed to manifest the "Thirty-two Physical Signs of the Buddhahood," such as the curl of white hair between his eyebrows from which he sends forth a ray of light to illuminate eighteen-thousand worlds, as he does in the *Lotus Sutra*.[2] More specifically, one of the thirty-two describes a male anatomy. So long as a woman can never hope to be equipped with all of the signs, it is logically impossible for her to become a Buddha. Also, sutras depict the Buddha Land as without women, though the purpose is to illustrate the belief that no distinction of any kind exists there.[3]

Nichiren (1222–1282, the fiery founder of the Nichiren Sect based on exclusive worship of the *Lotus Sutra*) wrote in a letter addressed to the Nun Sennichi: "Inasmuch as the *Lotus Sutra* confirms woman's Buddhahood, notwithstanding the denial by all other sutras, the women of Japan will be able to attain Buddhahood."[4] He is referring to Chapter 12 of the *Lotus Sutra*, "The Daughter of the Dragon-king Sagara." This episode is suspected to be a later interpolation, but it has nonetheless provided the foundation for the Mahayana position accepting woman's Buddhahood as possible. When disciples demand to see the proof of woman's potential, the Buddha sends for the daughter of the dragon king. She, "suddenly transformed into a male, perfect in Bodhisattva-deeds, sat on a precious lotus-flower attaining perfect enlightenment, with the Thirty-two Signs and the Eighty Kinds of Excellence, and universally proclaiming the Wonderful Law to every living creature in the world."[5] Nichiren declared, "The dragon daughter's attainment of Buddhahood betokens that of all women of all times."[6]

The *yamauba* wanders in absolute solitude through mountains, an unconquerable spirit with the ultimate willpower, a male symbol. In her knowledge that all things are equal and identical in their emptiness, she achieves a state of freedom where all distinctions vanish. She is no longer a woman and thus salvation is possible for her. In fact, she becomes a demon, transcending the human level. Similarly, the beautiful maiden in *Dōjōji* turns into a snake (a smaller version of a dragon) in her frenzied love, burns in the flames bursting from her own mouth, and finally achieves salvation when she leaps into the river while monks chant prayers on her behalf.[7] Tatsu (whose name means "dragon") and Tae (Virtuous Beauty) also achieve an eternal and supreme state after their living bodies as women are eliminated. The leper and the statue are, as it were, Rohan's metaphors for transfigured women readied for the final attainment of Buddhahood.

In a light satirical work, "The True Beauty" (1889), Rohan mocks the corrupt world in need of spiritual love. A man writes a letter to the Bodhisattva Kannon and the Emperor of Heaven demanding that they send a true beauty to save the people of Japan, for a true beauty, being a personification of the Buddha, has the power to humanize and purify crude men. He reproaches the deities: "If a true beauty descends upon us in this glorious Meiji period . . . , Japan will turn into a paradise. Why do you tarry in sending one to us? Today we are overrun by porcine and rodent women, and females resembling ducks and woodpeckers are having their day" (I, 207–208). He concludes his letter with the ultimatum: "If you should fail to respond to my request, I am determined to challenge you to a duel." According to the instructions given by Kannon's apparition, he dispatches an innkeeper to search in the mountains.

The innkeeper returned to report: "In the depths of woods, a beauty appeared in my path. Her walk was so elegant, her natural grace untainted by the evil winds of the world, and her charm overwhelming. She aroused a flame of emotion even in this old heart of mine. As I approached, she silently smiled with her graceful eyes, making my body and soul tremble as if being swept away in a misty spring breeze."

The man anxiously asked for her name and address. The innkeeper said: "I also asked the same question. Without words, she pointed to her sash. There it was, clearly engraved on a golden tag, 'So-and-so's daughter, So-and-so, born in 1886.'"

"What?" exclaimed the man. "A four-year-old? A true beauty!" (I, 207–208)

The burden of the flesh is such in reality that only a child can be in a state of purity and holiness. It comes to mind that the daughter of the dragon king in the *Lotus Sutra* was just eight years old.

Such a separation of body and soul as well as negation of the physical aspect of woman culminated in "Enlightenment of Love" (1891). It is a monologue of a man who has found himself in a prison of love, where he is not free even to hate his prison guard who is his beloved. He realizes that his arch enemy is his own body, which ties him to the world of illusion (reality). He had fallen in love with her because of her gentle nature, her all-embracing capacity for love, and her hands which know, not how to strike, but only how to comfort. He notes, "She rejoices to see the ignorant enlightened, while I only witness angels turn into devils; and she sojourns in the world of Goodness, Beauty, and Greatness, while I live in the world of blood, sweat, and tears" (I, 45). She loves him as she does a beggar, a blind man, or a convict working by the roadside. Her love has tamed the beast in him, and in this prison of love, not only his body but also his heart is no longer his own. She is like the sun, too bright for his eyes to behold, and her physical features are beyond his perception. He comes to learn that the true prison is not a punishment for evil deeds but rather a "sacred insulator" shielding the prisoner from the devil's bewitching beam. But he cannot confide his love to her, for pure love is without words, as a clear sky is without clouds. She falls ill and dies, leaving him in the prison of love for eternity.[8] He ends his monologue with a revelation: "This place called prison is actually a paradise where I can stroll hand in hand with her. This is Paradise, the one without the snake" (I, 47). This is love as a spiritual yearning and a means of self-cultivation. The girl is the eternal woman, Madonna as well as Eve, and the bodhisattva. Such love is, says Rohan, a religious impulse, which leads to love of all existences.

On the third level, Rohan clearly equates love with philosophical concepts—Buddhist compassion, Confucian humanity, Taoist acceptance of all things, and Christian love. In an article called "Love" (1940), he discusses related Japanese words such as *megumu* ("be merciful," "loving"), *megushi* ("lovely," "pitiful"), *mugoshi* ("tragic," "cruel"), *kanashi* ("beloved," "sad," "touching"), *kanashimu* ("grieve," "cherish"), *aware* ("pathos"), and *awaremu* ("love," "sympathize"). Rohan explains that the feeling underlying all these terms is *ai* ("love"), the character for which is shared by all of the above-mentioned words, except *mugoshi* (XXV, 664–65). When love intensifies, it brings tears to one's eyes; and when one sees the suffering of one's beloved, one cannot help but find it cruel. Rohan contends that the word *mugoshi* is thus related deeply to the emotion of love. *Ji* of *jihi* (Buddhist compassion) refers to the undiscriminating love for all, and *hi* is the grief and compassion shared by all suffering beings for one another; *jihi*, therefore, is profound love based on the universal knowledge of impermanence and the fundamental sadness of life.[9] Rohan further proceeds to prove that the character *ai* has yet another reading, *utsukushimu* ("cherish," "love"), the adjectival of which is *utsukushi* ("beautiful," "beloved"), obviously relating love to beauty.

Also in Japanese, the reading *chi* applies to the characters for milk, blood, and spirit. In Rohan's view, the most basic form of love is that between mother and child (or a wet nurse and her charge), which joins the physical and the spiritual, links the present and the past, and unites man with fellowmen. Wisdom is called "the Mother of all Buddhas," symbolized by the Mother Tārā in Tantric Buddhism. Wisdom as *pāramitā* refers to the bodhisattva practices, and as *prajñā*, it means the knowledge of emptiness, by the power of which man can transcend attachments and all distinctions to practice love of all things. On this level, therefore, Rohan sees woman as the symbol of both *agape* ("divine love") and *eros* ("human love") such as personified by Tae and Tatsu. Thus, love is, in Rohan's belief, the only key to self-cultivation, universal purification, and eventually, salvation.

IV *Art as Religious Practice*

If man is in reality constantly frustrated in his attempt to free himself from his own desires and outside pressures, it is natural that not all men are capable of achieving enlightenment through religious discipline. A humanist, Rohan found another way, just as difficult and effective, to arrive at the same end. For him, the purifier of mankind is the poet, that is, the creator—the artist and artisans. An artistic accomplishment demands absolute concentration, ceaseless self-improvement, courageous belief in man's capability, and sincere dedication, just as is required by religious discipline. Rohan's disciple Tamura Shōgyo once witnessed Rohan pondering all night long over one passage with such concentration that it had the appearance of aesthetic *zazen* ("meditation"), almost approaching a religious practice.[10] Rohan asserts that the fundamental attitude of artist is to be "as receptive as an ocean accepting all rivers..., and expressive or contributory as sweet rain falling on all things" (XXIV, 294), for only after forsaking one's own small ego can one attain the universal, greater ideal.

Artistic endeavor involves painful processes, racked by self-doubt and a feeling of helplessness. In the first of Rohan's artisan stories, "A Sword," Shōzō the swordsmith is reduced to making farm implements after he eloped with Ran, forsaking a promising job. A lord hears of his boastful claim to fine craftsmanship and orders a sword worthy of his ownership. When Shōzō confesses his incompetence to Ran, she deserts him, taking with her the fifty *ryō* given by the lord as the first payment. Forsaken and publicly ridiculed by his own wife, Shōzō at first cringes at the command of his lord:

I will never be able to do it. May my body be ground into powder to scatter in four winds! May my life be snuffed out like a smoke! I have no hope of receiving divine protection: the rain of my sins will pour down on me even through the cover of the divine tree, and the black clouds of my evil deeds will shield the light of Mercy from me. Let me die! Oh, the wind of the empty space, turn into poison to kill this sinful man! (V, 42)

As he picks up a sickle and tries to pierce his belly, however, a thought occurs to him: "Who were those that made the

renowned swords of the past? Not demons nor bodhisattvas.
I am a man just as much as those swordsmiths before me. I
shall not die, no, not in vain! Born a man in this divine country
of ours, why should I die like a worm?" (V, 46).

Rohan is successful when he chooses artist-artisans for his
heroes: for one reason, art in the medieval age required a unity
of spirit and skill, and the way of the artist-artisan involved
an all-or-nothing risk. A great master's professional secret was
not communicated verbally, for it was transmittable only through
intuition, much like religious insight. The true test of his
accomplishment, then, does not rest in the judgment of others
but in the artist himself and the challenge from the higher
order. (Shu'un risks his own existence as a man and a Buddhist
sculptor to pour his entire life force into creating a perfect
work of art—the love bodhisattva, but not to please human eyes.)
Having overcome his sense of inadequacy, Shōzō succeeds in
producing a splendid sword, almost with a life of its own,
like a manifestation of a divine dragon. In the final scene
of "A Sword":

> The lord said, "Well done, Shōzō! This is indeed a magnificent
> work. But this sword looks too exquisite to be dependable. How
> serviceable is it?"
> Before the lord could utter another word, Shōzō leapt upon the
> veranda and stood erect like a deva king. Striking his enormous
> abdomen, he exclaimed: "Try it right here, and you shall see me
> halved before your eyes!" (V, 46)

Eliminating all other thoughts from his mind, Shōzō was able
to elevate himself onto the veranda inaccessible to commoners.

This tale shows the typical merits and flaws of Rohan's early
idealistic stories in which characters are embodiments of
Rohan's ideals, lacking in psychological depth or individuality
yet memorable for their sincerity and passionate determination.
Characterization is rather implausible, turning a slothful, indecisive, abject Shōzō abruptly into a dedicated, self-confident,
superexcellent swordsmith. It took Rohan a few more months
and a spiritual crisis to surmount such imperfections and mature
his techniques.

CHAPTER 4

The Value Crisis

I *Pursuit of* fūryū

IN July, 1890, Rohan was living in retreat away from the heat and clamor of Tokyo. He was in the throes of serious doubt over the intrinsic value of fiction: as long as a work of fiction is born of creative imagination, is it not essentially spurious and nugatory? Despondent and in a wretched mood, Rohan confesses his crisis as a writer in a famous letter known as the "Jigokudani (Hell Valley) epistle" to Tsubouchi Shōyō:

Since I began to engage in literary pursuits, I have aspired to attain *fūryū* with all my being. . . . But I found the path of *fūryū* suddenly blocked by a great river without a ferry. Now I know that it was simply for the lack of genuine insight into the spirit of *fūryū* that I had been content to interpret *fūryū* merely as "emotion in harmony with reason.". . . I am in despair to realize that my past endeavors in writing fiction have been absolutely un-*fūryū*. I am losing the courage to pick up my pen because I shall create a devilish world of untruth in my state of un-*fūryū*.[1]

The word *fūryū* frequently appeared in the titles of Edo popular literature, indicating "amorous, worldly, elegant" among other nebulous meanings. Of modern writers Rohan is by far the most conspicuous in its use. In fact, the entire plot of "Dewdrops" leads up to the matter of *fūryū*, for Bunseimu's primary purpose in advertising for a man who never fails to be cheerful is to find a companion to accompany him on a *fūryū* journey. The Japanese poet who is finally chosen is a man of *fūryū*, for he wants nothing, owns nothing, but lives in a carefree, therefore, perfect world of his own. Thus, Rohan's *fūryū* begins with a state unhindered, unattached, and free of

59

care. Bunseimu amassed his fortune not through financial manipu-
lation but by way of rigorous labor (in the whaling business),
and he has come to be a man of *fūryū*, for whom wealth is not
an end in itself. For Rohan, evil was not material wealth but
rather materialism, or being a slave to wealth. Scientific progress
and material prosperity may in fact be of help in achieving
enlightenment, or they may result from enlightenment: even
a bed of grass feels as comfortable as a silk brocade mattress
to an enlightened person. (Thus, Tae living in her humble
hut can surprise Young Rohan in "Encounter With a Skull" by
the unexpected opulence of her bedding.)

Fūryū in modern usage means "tasteful, artistic, refined, and
poetic." In a short article "On Taste" (1912), Rohan defines
taste as one's insight, belief, dignity, and character. Taste, as
he saw it, meant a free state of mind without attachment or
care but with a capacity for infinite pleasure. Around 1890 to
1891, a group of about ten men met occasionally to enjoy
transcendental talk, drinks, and excursions together in the
spirit of *fūryū*. They were all residents of the Negishi and
Yanaka areas in Tokyo, and the group is commonly known as
the Negishi group (*Negishi-ha*) by literary historians. They
included writers, artists, critics, with Okakura Tenshin (1862–
1913, art historian and the curator of the Oriental Division of
the Boston Museum) as an associate member. Rohan was the
youngest among them but edited the first and only issue of
their journal called *Kyōgen Kigo* (Make-believe Witticism). This
group represented an innocent, romantic aspect of *fūryū* in the
tradition of Taoist sages meeting in the bamboo forests to
engage in spiritual talk away from the philistine world.

Man's taste, on the other hand, had a more serious aspect
for Rohan. *Shumi*, which is usually translated as "avocation,"
can be a sacred vocation on which some men would stake their
lives. Rohan expressed an enormous admiration for Sen no
Rikyū (1522–1591), the greatest master of the tea ceremony,
who chose death by ritual disembowelment rather than to
compromise his inner and artistic freedom under the pressure
of Toyotomi Hideyoshi (1538–1598, a powerful ruler of unified
Japan). *Fūryū* at this point ceases to be an avocation, for a
man's entire existence depends on it, when he has reached the

ultimate stage of *fūryū*—true freedom. Rohan compares Rikyū to Taoist immortals in "Antiques" (1920): by elevating the status of tea ceremony, Rikyū created gold (money value) out of base material (tea cups and pots), though the resultant financial gains were enjoyed solely by Hideyoshi (VI, 347). The central concept in the tea ceremony and haiku—the most representative of tasteful pursuits—is *fūryū*. "Rikyū's Wife" (1913) describes the remarkable unity of an aged couple. Rikyū, who attained the profoundest secret of spiritual perfection through the tea ceremony,[2] is examining an incense burner. His wife joins him in the contemplation. There is a mysterious understanding without utterance, whereupon she observes, "The legs of the burner seem a tenth of an inch too long." "I thought exactly the same," smiles Rikyū. They are united in true and blissful harmony. "They were husband and wife with not a tenth of an inch difference in their discerning taste" (VI, 56), marvels Rohan at the end. Rikyū and his wife are able to attain spiritual union through the tea ceremony, because true *fūryū* is a universal state—a form of perfection for Rohan.

To the humanist Rohan, *fūryū* meant being truly human. Consequently, *fūryū* embraces the emotion of love: A man of *fūryū* is an artist who loves and glorifies man. When an artist is successful, his work of art inevitably comes to life, as do the statue of bodhisattva as warm as a girl in the flesh and the pagoda standing firm like a deva king. Rohan's love is a universal, infinite, and quintessential love, attainable only through unmitigated devotion. Love can be an obstacle in the path toward consummate freedom, but man without love is not human. Shu'un, therefore, does not strive to overcome his love but rather to purify and sublimate it. When he succeeds, his work becomes the ideal woman and a bodhisattva, a religious object as well as a work of art. More significantly, since the deified Tatsu ascends to heaven as Shu'un's wife, she still retains human relationships. The ideal state of *fūryū*, then, is the unity of love, faith, and beauty (art), through which man can achieve salvation. Such a concept is by no means unique, for the West has its Pygmalion legend, the *Divine Comedy*, and *Faust*, while in the Japanese literary tradition the belief that artistic sensitivity can spiritualize love has been the basic assumption in the theory of *mono no aware* ("pathos of things").[3]

In the Jigokudani letter, Rohan confesses that unable to find genuine literary *fūryū* except in the later poems of Bashō (the most celebrated haiku poet), he has concluded that one can create superior works only if one lives in absolute reality; and one cannot call himself a true poet until one has become a sage at the same time.[4] Finally, Rohan defines *fūryū* as elimination of delusions before all else. Here his concept of *fūryū* borders on both a religious state and a poetic state: true *fūryū* must by nature aspire toward the ultimate Buddhahood and must have the power to save mankind. That is why the Buddhist sculptor Shu'un pursues his artistic training with a solemn determination as if it were religious discipline and succeeds in sublimating his love and art into a religion.

II *The Heart Sutra Commentary*

In August, 1890 also at Jigokudani, Rohan wrote "A Commentary on the Secondary Meaning of the Heart Sutra." He never attempted to publish it, but fortunately the manuscript was preserved by a disciple and published after Rohan's death. "The secondary meaning" implies that a commentary can only be an expedient to help perceive true meaning, for the true meaning of sutras is transmittable only through a language without words, that is, through action. The full title of this sutra is *Maka Hannya Haramitsuta Shin-gyō* (*Mahā Prajñāpāramitā hridaya Sutra*). *Maka* (*mahā*) means "great, profound." *Hannya* (*prajñā*) refers to transcendental insight, or the mental operation through which the mind judges good and evil and eradicates false attachments. *Haramitsuta* (*pāramitā*) is the ultimate means, or knowledge of the eternal truth, which immediately leads to enlightenment; and therefore it also means the achievement of enlightenment, that is, the arrival at the Ideal Sphere of Truth. Finally, *shin* means "essence, heart." In English, this sutra is usually rendered as the Heart Sutra, or the Essence of Profound Wisdom and Enlightenment Sutra.

This sutra consists of two hundred and sixty-five Chinese characters in the text translated by Hsuan-tsang (602–664) of the T'ang Dynasty. Not only is this the shortest of sutras, but it came into being in a unique manner. A body of literature referred to as the Great *Prajñāpāramitā* (*Dai-hannya*) encompasses six hundred volumes of sutras which fall into two hundred and sixty-five parts. The Heart Sutra is a composite of words (or characters) selected one from each of these parts: hence, the essence (heart) of *Prajñāpāramitā*. Rohan's commentary states that the essence of the six hundred volumes of the Great *Prajñāpāramitā* is condensed into the Heart Sutra, the nucleus of which is found in the twenty-four characters: "matter is no different from emptiness, and emptiness is no different from matter. Matter is emptiness, and emptiness is matter. So it is also with perception, intellection, action, and reason."

The best-known words in the Heart Sutra are *shiki soku ze kū* ("matter is emptiness"), which Rohan interprets to mean that things do not *become* empty but *are* empty fundamentally and eternally, just as a rainbow exists yet is materially empty. It is not that a rainbow disappears and becomes empty, but rather that it is empty in itself, for it is merely an incorporeal phenomenon resulting from a temporary relationship between vapor and sunlight. When a man realizes that his own body, which is the source of all his desires and suffering, is also merely a phenomenon produced by the workings of multiple relationships (*innen*) and human actions (*karma*), he will be freed from suffering. The Heart Sutra declares empty all the Twelve Causes and Effects (*jūni innen*)—a vicious cycle starting with Ignorance, Past Action, and ending with Present Action, Life, Old Age, and Death: if Ignorance is empty, void, nonexistent, then there can be no karma, no future life, and no death. The Heart Sutra concludes that *prajñāpāramitā* (insight and knowledge which eliminate the first cause, Ignorance) is the supreme and sublime magic formula to eradicate all suffering. In fact, its Japanese translation, *Hannya haramitsu!*, is sometimes chanted in place of the more common *Namu Amidabutsu* or *Namu Myōhōrenge-kyō* to dispel adverse luck.

Inasmuch as Buddhism places the primary emphasis on action, *pāramitā* also involves bodhisattva practices, including perseverance, assiduous endeavor, concentration, self-discipline, concern for others, and insight (which are generally called the Six *Pāramitā*). The last eighteen characters of the Heart Sutra represent a magic spell (*dhārani*), which is rendered in Sanskrit as "*gate, gate, pāragate, para saṁgate, bodhi svāhā*" in the latest translation of the Heart Sutra by Garma C. C. Chang in his *The Buddhist Teaching of Totality* (1971). Japanese scholars generally translate it to mean, "When you have arrived, when you and others together have arrived at the Other Shore, there will be enlightenment; there will be attainment."[5] Suzuki Daisetsu's rather loose translation (*Manual of Zen Buddhism*, 1935), on the other hand, is in the past tense: "O, Bodhi, gone, gone, gone to the other shore, landed at the other shore. Svāhā!" The uniqueness of Rohan's interpretation is that he takes the entire passage to be in the imperative form: "Depart, depart, to the Other Shore! All together depart to the Other Shore! Swiftly on the Only Way!" (XL, 102–103). Thus, in Rohan's eyes, the essence of the Heart Sutra lies as much in urging man to strive resolutely and promptly toward universal enlightenment as in the revelation of the principle of emptiness, with the knowledge of which man must ceaselessly endeavor to help others so that all mankind can attain salvation at once.

Rohan, however, warns against the danger of incomplete knowledge: *Prajñā* is like a sharp sword—if a man misuses the knowledge of emptiness to indulge in hedonistic disregard of basic human obligations, for example, it is as if he had committed moral suicide. In the same text, Rohan quotes Bashō's ironic haiku, "How holy! / A man who is not enlightened / By every flash of lightning," as a pungent admonition against false awakening and a self-deceptive sense of accomplishment. Too readily achieved awakening is a pseudoenlightenment which does more harm than good to oneself and others. Rohan confesses that he himself used to enjoy futile contemplation in a hermitage and indulge in the folly of reading sutras while drinking saké until fortunately he was awakened by the cold realization that life was "empty."

He erred, admits Rohan in retrospect, because he was exclusively concerned with *shiki soku ze kū* ("matter is emptiness"), overlooking the next passage in the Heart Sutra, *kū soku ze shiki* ("emptiness is matter"). He marvels at the ingenuity of the sutra in first breaking down the illusion of the physical aspects of existence only to reconstruct the phenomenal reality again. Inasmuch as "emptiness is matter" is also the truth, man must accept his own corporeal entity, empty as it is, to live, suffer, love, and hate as a man. Rohan notes that a man experiences displeasure and anguish so long as he is attached to his own self, mistaking the mass of flesh as himself. Man must destroy this illusion of his existence with the sword of *prajñā* (transcendental insight to perceive the principle of emptiness), Rohan advises, and his world will turn into a paradise where the only and true sorrow is the infinite sorrow of the bodhisattva for the suffering of mankind. The meaning of man's existence, then, hangs on the concept of emptiness.

Emptiness (*sūnyatā*) is similar to the mathematical concept of zero: zero as nothingness is the ultimate negation of all things; yet it is the point from which infinite numbers originate. Emptiness, similarly, is by no means a logic of nihilism but absolute transcendentalism and a lofty vision symbolizing the magnitude of potential functions. As zero remains zero after being multiplied by whatever number, so can emptiness contain infinite things and still remain empty. Emptiness is explained from three points of view by Frederick Streng. Epistemologically, emptiness is enlightenment, for it enables man to avoid the sorrow resulting from a state of ignorance. From a psychological standpoint, emptiness is freedom from existence and self, or a feeling of bliss. On a cosmological level, emptiness means relatedness of all existing things: since everything is void of an absolute nature and therefore dependent, the ultimate wisdom must be "perfect comprehension of the relationship between those who suffer, the suffering, and the alleviation of suffering."[6]

Modern Buddhist scholars go further in their interpretation of emptiness. Kino Kazuyoshi agrees that "matter is emptiness" means that all things are empty, but speculates that the emptiness in "emptiness is matter" is equivalent to what can be called the unfathomably expansive life of the Buddha. When man learns the emptiness of his own petty existence, he would find himself living within the embrace of the vast Buddha life. That state, suggests Kino, is "emptiness is matter."[7] Elsewhere Rohan also expressed a similar idea in regard to the Taoist way to immortality (*sendō*). In producing an elixir of immortality, a Taoist acquires a life other than his original self, says Rohan, for he becomes one with the universe to transcend life and death (XVIII, 489–90). It would not be farfetched to compare such a view to that of St. Paul, who felt after the Resurrection that he no longer lived but rather Christ lived within him. In fact, Rohan, in the same text, often compares Taoist concepts to Christian beliefs.

The principle of emptiness in the Heart Sutra is, of course, vastly different from nihilism. It is the ultimate knowledge indispensable in achieving psychological detachment and religious awakening, which in turn are essential to the bodhisattva practices. The Slight-No-One Bodhisattva (see Chapter 6, section III) is said to have heard on his deathbed the Lotus Sutra being preached to him by a mysterious voice in the air.[8] The final stage of the bodhisattva practice is reached when all things are completely empty; even the Law is empty, as the Heart Sutra reveals. Rohan once wrote a poem on the meaning of "matter is emptiness":

Iwa ni kudake	Notwithstanding the sound
Nagisa ni yosuru	Of breaking against rocks
Oto wa are	And rippling over the beach,
Mizu o hanarete	There could be no waves
Tatsu nami mo nashi.	Apart from the water.
	(XL, 31)

This poem suggests the following: the Law is like the sound in being devoid of substance, and physical identities such as human beings are but waves to communicate the Law, as invisible and elusive as the sound in space; the differentiated reality of phenomena cannot exist apart from water—a Kegon symbol of the undifferentiated reality (the world of principle); in human terms, moreover, man's individuality (water) in its action (waves) carries out or proclaims the truth of existence symbolized by the incorporeal sound, for the mind or insight can function only when it is fused with the body (matter) in temporary relationship—as soon as the relationship is dissolved, there will be no matter, no mental activity, no insight, no mind, and all will be empty. It is Rohan's belief that while man exists, nevertheless, he undeniably is charged with a definite function and an all-surpassing purpose, which leave him no time for pessimistic despair.

As seen from Rohan's own agonizing contemplation in solitude, the pursuit of *fūryū* is a desperate, painful, and horrifying process. Rohan's *fūryū* requires, first of all, a confrontation with the evil in oneself before elimination of delusions can be accomplished; and therefore, *fūryū* is a momentous, life-and-death combat at the risk of self-extinction rather than a simple escape from worldly cares. Unlike the universal drama of the fight between Good and Evil over the possession of a human soul, it is similar to Zen contemplation, in which one must negate and eliminate all concepts as delusions in order to perceive the emptiness. It is an inescapable and fierce struggle of a soul trying to save itself.

III *Warning against Indulgence*

Upon returning from Jigokudani, Rohan shaved his head like a monk in repentance of his past state of un-*fūryū* and also in his determination to pursue *fūryū* unhindered by worldly pretence. The first work to appear after his homecoming was "A Sealed Letter" (1890), in which Rohan describes the horrendous visions that may well reflect his own inner experiences at Jigokudani.

A man called Genkō (Illusory Hook) is meditating in his hermitage named the Demon's Den. His young daughter comes to him with a letter from her dead mother. He ignores her completely, leaving her standing outside in a severe snowstorm. Suddenly she vanishes, and a demon materializes before Genkō to read aloud the letter in which Genkō's wife confesses her burning love for him and introduces their daughter as a living proof of their former evil deed, that is, their marriage. Love is traditionally condemned as an evil deed in Buddhist views, for it is a formidable obstacle in achieving freedom from attachment. Moving this argument a step further here, Rohan is suggesting that a child who issued from the parents' act of love is in a sense decisive evidence condemning the parents. But Genkō's wife vows to become a demon to destroy anyone who would erase the memory of "their shame"—the daughter. Genkō sits in deep meditation, refusing to allow memories of love to disturb his mind. But a simple refusal to accept the past is not enough to save him from a deadly ordeal.

Finishing the letter, the demon pulled Genkō upside down by his legs, tore him to bits, and devoured him to the last drop of blood. No sooner was he consumed in agony than the demon was changed into Genkō only to be eaten by another demon in turn. Bones and entrails crunched under powerful fangs.... What agony to be slowly torn apart, tormented, and chewed again and again! There was no end to the cycle and no pause for breath. With his tears exhausted and his tongue too stiff to cry out, Genkō's mind suffered interminable torture. (I, 442)

A cold gust of wind awakens Genkō. Soon rugged mountains converge on the little hut from all sides.

Walls crumbled, posts collapsed, everything inside was smashed. Genkō was jammed between rocks, unable to move his limbs—his neck was caught twisted; his body was racked in pain, barely breathing, powerless to budge. The rocks around him grew hot, blazing hot. Ferocious flames and smoke burst forth from all sides to incinerate Genkō. His skin dissolved, hair was singed, flesh melted, bones flamed. Then he was ashes. (I, 444)

After writhing through the same cycle over and over again, he realizes that his denial of all past deeds was as sinful as his original enjoyment of lustful pleasure in his unenlightened life. The story concludes: "'I censure myself and trust in Heaven,' Genkō declared and serenely resumed his reading. There will be times, no doubt, when he is again torn apart by demons and crushed by mountains" (I, 448).

The horrors of the consequences of evildoing and the contemptible corruption of the depraved are described also in Rohan's satires, in which he tries more explicitly to persuade the reader that he would do well to avoid evil. Most of his works in this category are quite humorous as well as hortatory. Rohan's laughter, however, is not the derisive expression of a self-righteous moralist or a cynic; rather, it derives from intel-

lectual understanding that laughter is man's safety valve. In
an article discussing humorous stories, Rohan compares sincere
tears to the "pure water flowing in the deep valley of human
emotion" and rightful wrath to the "furious heat from a flaming
sense of justice." Then, he reflects that "true laughter is like a
charming and mysterious flower blooming out of a harmonious
union of tears and wrath"; and "a mountain is as tall as its
valley is deep, and so genuine laughter is possible only through
comprehension of profound suffering" (XV, 820–22). By suffering, of course, he refers to the Buddhist concept of deep sorrow
for the suffering of all sentient beings, not simply one's own
personal suffering.

In the "Preface to Demon of Lust" (1890), Rohan warns
against indulgence in lust—the chief cause of human miseries—
by illustrating its devastating effects on a man. A wealthy
father, alarmed by the degeneration of his eight sons, sets up
a sort of diorama to admonish them. As the viewers walk
through from booth to booth arranged much like a fun house
at an amusement center, they see in the first booth a profligate
surrounded by attractive figures representing courtesans. The
second shows him at a sumptuous banquet, and the next three
depict the profligate merrymaking in a courtesan's chamber.
In the sixth, however, he is rebuked and disinherited by his
father. He appears as a pauper in the seventh, and in the
following two booths he is suffering from venereal disease. In
the tenth, he is revoltingly disfigured, and in the eleventh he
exhibits the symptoms of the last syphilitic phase. In the last
booth, the viewers find themselves tripping over the man's skull
in a bleak field. The show is entirely successful in its aim: since
its opening, no customer has dared to visit the gay quarters.
The authorities eventually close the show at the request of the
brothel owners, and the wealthy man becomes a saintly hermit.
A writer called Rohan happens to meet him and decides to
carry out the same mission through his own writings.

Most works of this type are products of Rohan's early period,
when he was seized by a burning sense of mission to lead
the people to self-purification. His attack on the evils of the
world and human hypocrisy is charged with uncompromising
wrath and acrid irony. If he resembles Saikaku in his descriptions

of the "floating world," it is as a sober critic of the sinful ways of that world, quite unlike Kōyō, who was intoxicated by Saikaku's amorous world and described it for its own sake. Rohan depicted outlandishly amorous scenes merely as a means to bring on catharsis and eventual enlightenment.

In "Instructions of an Old Profligate" (1891), an old man advises a young woman on thirty-five techniques of love. He lists the ways to catch a man, keep his interest, and discreetly drop him should he fall into adverse circumstances (due to business failure, disinheritance, or simple exhaustion of his financial resources). When it comes to the eight infallible techniques of lovemaking, apparently reminiscent of the *Kama Sutra*, he gives no details beyond their enigmatic names, declaring them to be the profoundest secrets which deserve additional fees. Even so, Rohan's preface reveals that the original manuscript was repeatedly rejected by publishers for fear of official and public censure. Rohan decided to revise and publish it in the belief that in reading it even if only to criticize, people might discern his serious intent and accept it as the sincere advice of a good friend. At the beginning and the end, the old man repeatedly reminds the woman that the key to the entire operation in love is male vanity, and warns her that if a woman should fall into the same pitfall of self-conceit, the techniques he prescribes will have no effect. Such tongue-in-cheek sketches of slice-of-life scenes contributed to Rohan's experiments in realistic techniques.

Late in 1890, Rohan joined the *Kokkai* newspaper, a subsidiary of the *Asahi*, to remain until it was dissolved in 1895. Quite well paid as a staff novelist, he was able to work with considerable financial and psychological security. The first major work to appear in the *Kokkai* was "The Wandering Balladeer," followed by its sequel "Surprise Gunshot." A Kyoto smith called Torakichi goes bankrupt through his indulgence in wine, women, and *jōruri* ("ballad chanting"). He makes his way to Edo as a street balladeer, is discovered by a retired *daimyo*, and hired as an entertainer in residence. In the sequel, Torakichi, in his new and more fashionable name, Dōya, is ordered to manufacture guns for Lord Shimazu. He succeeds with his bold imagination and resourcefulness and enjoys the prestigious status of exclusive purveyor. Again he indulges in sensuous pleasures, with a courtesan and a samurai's daughter competing for his love. Wealthy, influential, and vainglorious, he visits his former Kyoto colleagues, who are dazzled by his good fortune. There is, however, one old smith who remains unimpressed, reaffirming the traditional pride of the medieval artisan, and refuses to kowtow to the power of Dōya's wealth.

In these two works, Rohan tries to describe the actions of the characters for their own sake rather than merely to illustrate his philosophy. The transformation of the protagonist is neither instantaneous nor unequivocal. Torakichi must experience humiliation, deprivation, and suffering before he is saved by virtue of his dignity, which remains intact. Yet the primary theme of these two tales is not the simple conversion of a profligate into an intrepid and productive man: the descriptions of Torakichi's demeaning journey command the major portion of "The Wandering Balladeer"; and "Surprise Gunshot" devotes ninety percent of its space to Dōya's frolicking and vain show of success. In this first attempt to use a realistic approach, Rohan chose as his subject the conflict between man and materialism, in which even a man of dauntless spirit might become reduced to a self-indulgent mediocrity—a familiar hero in Saikaku's amorous (*kōshoku*) tales. Rohan's real ideal is undoubtedly the spirit of the lone old smith called Jōshu (Pure Jewel), but it is also evident that Rohan was intrigued by the personality of talented, versatile Dōya, who has the self-awareness and aggressive will of the Meiji man in contrast to his passive, self-destructive, effeminate Genroku counterpart. Rohan's style is less poetic and forceful here than in his previous works, and these two stories are probably the last manifestation of Saikaku's stylistic influence on Rohan.

At this point, Rohan was about to enter into his most productive period, armed with the experience in realistic techniques and the new realization (a result of the Jigokudani contemplation) that literature must be an expression or an embodiment of something most solemn, everlasting, universal, and vital: that is, the true human existence within eternal cosmos.

CHAPTER 5

The Culmination

I The Whaler *and Karma*

IN 1891, Rohan wrote two major works: *The Whaler*, the only one of his three long novels to be completed; and "The Five-storied Pagoda," perhaps his greatest accomplishment.

The Whaler is the life story of Hikoemon, a farmer's son. He leaves his home in Izu Province at the age of fourteen and works faithfully as a dyer's apprentice in Kyoto. A handsome and bright boy, he is seduced into an illicit affair by his master's neglected wife. Exceedingly moral in character, he is unable to live with his conscience and flees westward, eventually to reach Kyushu and become a whaler. While he is living an exhilarating masculine life among the jovial whalers, he gets married and fathers a son. This peaceful life comes to an end when he discovers his wife's adulterous affair and kills her, her lover, and even her aged mother, who arranged the clandestine meeting. He fails in a suicide attempt and drifts out toward Korea in a small boat. Almost drowned in a storm, finally he reaches the Island of Iki, where he meets a wise old man who owns the whaling rights on the island. Hikoemon confesses what he has done and the old man instructs him in moral obligation and acceptance of fate, counselling him to live his life out in good faith. Hikoemon works hard as a harpooner for ten years and accumulates a considerable sum of money. After the death of his benefactor, Hikoemon returns to his home province, settles down as an influential landlord, and remarries. Years later he meets a naval officer and recognizes the young man to be his son by his first marriage, whom he had abandoned at sea, unable to kill an innocent infant by his own hand. The entire story is in the form of Hikoemon's confession to the son.

The most famous sections are the descriptions of the whalers' life, the scene of whale catching by premodern methods (perhaps the only one of its kind in Japanese literature), and the portentous apparitions of his victims haunting him in the violent sea storm. In *The Whaler*, Rohan's idealistic tendencies are beginning to blend with his attempts at objective and descriptive techniques. Characterization is more natural and plausible with a certain psychological depth; and the plot development is intricately related to the personality of each character involved. Hikoemon's extreme honesty leads him into a fight with a traveling companion who refuses to return a wallet they found to its rightful owner, but at the same time, Hikoemon finds employment with the dyer through a man who intercedes in the fight. Later, his chivalric spirit, which prompts him to rescue a man being beaten by a score of ruffians, also compels him to accept a marriage arranged by the grateful man. The treachery of Hikoemon's wife proves her own undoing: she hands over a hatchet to her lover, and her irate husband snatches it and kills them with it. And it is partly Hikoemon's sense of justice that causes him to spare his baby's life, saying, "You will come back to me some day, if you are ordained by fate to avenge your mother's death." But it leads to a happy reunion, proving the complete expiation, through a life of penitence, of all his sins born of his passionate nature.

To a great extent, this novel reveals Rohan's views on human nature and karma. The Buddhist term *karma* ("action") refers to the accumulation of all the actions that a man takes throughout his numerous incarnations. By *inga ōhō* (the law of cause and effect), one of the most popularly believed cycles in Buddhism, these actions inevitably affect his later lives. In philosophical terms, *karma* means the effect of a man's actions on his own life. *Nirvana* ("final release") is often conceived as the exhaustion of *karma*, which is the cause of suffering. One way of exhausting *karma* is inaction, or not creating any additional *karma*. And obviously, the opposite choice is to counteract the effects of negative *karma* by creating positive *karma*. Inasmuch as the law governing the direct relationship between cause and effect is incomprehensible to man, the passive method of inaction may be easier and safer. The humanist Rohan, who believed in the Buddha nature in every man, nevertheless advocated a life of positive action.

In a collection of short pieces called "A Garden of Tales" (1895), Rohan briefly discusses *unmei* ("karma," "fate"): "A great man with a mission to accomplish must have the determination to create his own fate, instead of blaming Fate" (XXIV, 152). It is in the mysterious interaction between human will and Fate that a novelist Rohan found the best subject matter for his fiction. Since, in the Buddhist law of cause and effect, it is man's own actions that serve as causes, man is very much responsible for his own fate. In "Love Bodhisattva," the sculptor Shu'un's total devotion to religious art and love enables him to break through his karma cycle to achieve salvation; and Tae's inescapable suffering and unintentional pilgrimage finally bring her to a realm of eternal contentment in "Encounter With a Skull."

In *The Whaler*, Rohan describes the vicissitudes of life not so much as records of particular events and people's lives as concrete examples to illustrate the workings of the law of cause and effect. In his view, fate is closely related to man's self-cultivation and almost equivalent to manifestation of man's will. The main messages conveyed in this novel are that the law of cause and effect exists as unequivocally and perceptibly as reality itself and that man must endure suffering by the strength of his will in order to turn adverse karma into good fortune.

In his essay, "On Endeavor" (1910), Rohan observes that a successful man interprets fate as his own power, and a failure sees himself as a pawn of Fate. He pronounces them both wrong, for fate and human power together determine man's state of being. Since Rohan believes in man's perfectibility (man is not all good but can be), he is positive that life can be improved and man can achieve salvation through extermination of evils in society and within himself. Rohan defines a hero as one who has a desire to control fate, rather than being controlled submissively, and in the end proves it possible by his own life. In discussing the relation of human power and fate, Rohan concludes that a great man is he who holds himself alone responsible, for the crucial test of greatness is whether he is willing to risk shedding his own blood or seeks only things soft and smooth to grasp (XXVII, 350–52).

Real life is nonetheless far from being so simple as to let every man achieve his goal. Gotō Chūgai (1866–1938), a scholarly critic and ardent admirer of Rohan, points out in his 1894 article that Rohan has a talent for illustrating how fate is determined by a man's character as well as by the law of cause and effect. Chūgai poses the following questions. A man born weak and talentless cannot expect to overcome his adverse karma to attain happiness on his own. Since a man is either weak or strong due to his inborn qualities, the issue narrows down to who holds the power to distribute such attributes. And what are the rules governing such distribution? Unless we can learn the answers, retribution is by no means just or appropriate, but simply accidental.[1] Chūgai turns to *The Whaler* for an example. Hikoemon is steadfast and exceedingly moral yet quite given to violent emotional outbursts, a certain sign of his passionate imagination. It is natural, then, that he succumbs to Shun's amorous advances, commits a crime of passion, and is haunted by the phantoms of his victims. Chūgai explains that Hikoemon's passionate, imaginative nature is the cause which, once triggered by chance contact with Shun's desire and his wife's infidelity, inevitably drives him to sinful acts.

As Chūgai noted, *The Whaler* is a remarkable work in which events are closely related to the personality traits of each character, and a reader can easily apply modern psychological analysis to the story. Chūgai, nevertheless, was mistaken in his somewhat Darwinian assumption. Rohan never postulated that a man was born weak or strong. Even Shun is driven to an adulterous relation with Hikoemon by her husband's jealous suspicion and his frequent visits to the gay quarters. And Hikoemon's wife happens to resume her love affair with her ex-husband, from whom she was once separated against her will and his. Far from being simplistic, Rohan observes life with penetrating yet sympathetic eyes, for in his view, the real human tragedy is not that a man may be born weak and beyond salvation but rather that he is desperately bound in the intricate and mysterious web woven by his own emotions and karma.

II *"The Five-storied Pagoda"*

Although Rohan's literary techniques had not yet fully matured, *The Whaler* shows a markedly improved unity of idealistic theme and realistic approach. Such changes in novelistic techniques culminated in creating his best work, "The Five-storied Pagoda." It was written while Rohan was residing in the Yanaka area (present Daitō-ku) in Tokyo, near Tennō Temple (formerly called Kannō Temple), whose five-storied, eighty-seven-foot-tall pagoda was visible when going in and out of Rohan's house. Unfortunately this pagoda (admired by other writers and poets in the area),[2] built originally in 1644 and reconstructed in 1791, was totally destroyed by fire as a result of a double suicide in 1957.

In the mid-1700s, a talented yet unknown carpenter-architect, nicknamed Jūbei the Slow-wit for his lack of worldly wisdom and tact, incurs animosity when he competes against his own master (Genta) over the construction of a pagoda. The eminent abbot of Kannō Temple intercedes by telling the two rivals a parable on the virtue of cooperation and compassion. Compromising in accord with conventional ethics, Genta suggests a joint venture, but Jūbei insists on all or nothing. After Jūbei receives the contract, an irate fellow carpenter attacks him with an adz, hacking his ear and shoulder. Jūbei's total dedication to his work undiminished by the serious injury finally wins the loyalty of his crew. While a fierce storm threatens the newly completed pagoda and Genta circles the ground in rain and wind, Jūbei stands on the top veranda ready to die should his work prove less than perfect in nature's test. At the dedication ceremony, the abbot inscribes: "Constructed by Jūbei, and perfected by Genta."

As others have already noted [comments Tsubouchi Shōyō], the structure of this story compares with the superb architecture of the very pagoda that the protagonist constructs. . . . Stylistically the most magnificent is Chapter 32, where the demons ravage the city. The final inscription by the Abbot Rōen seems to sum up the quintessence of the entire story, perhaps with a hidden moral precept.[3]

"The Five-storied Pagoda" is Rohan's best-known and most popular work. (It was translated into English by Shioya Sakae in 1909 and published in a limited edition by Ōkura Shoten in Tokyo as *The Pagoda* by Kōda Nariyuki.)[4] One reason for its popularity is that the storm scene was included in the Ministry of Education textbooks for almost half a century, making this work familiar and memorable to the hearts of all children.

The Exalted King Demon bellowed out in a ferocious voice: "Humans have held us in contempt too long.... Dogs that walk, instead of crawling; birds that made nests of extravagance and roosts of arrogance; monkeys without a tail; snakes that speak; sons of the fox without a shred of sincerity; female pigs without a sense of shame—how long can we tolerate their affront?... The ordained period of sixty-four years is over, and I have broken out of the Cave of Mercy and Forbearance that held us prisoners.... Applaud the schemes that humans thought were shrewd; praise their heart that they thought was noble; extol the emotions that they thought were beautiful; eulogize the truth that they thought was attained; and glorify their power that they thought was mighty.... Skin them alive, peel off their flesh, and make balls of their hearts to kick about...." The King Demon urged on without pause, arousing thousands of his kinsmen.

Those crossing the water stirred up waves, and those running over land kicked over sands. Heaven and earth turned yellow with dust until even the sun was obscured. Some swung axes, sneering as they felled pine trees carefully trimmed by men of taste. Some let spears dance swiftly to bore holes into wooden roofs. Others shook well-built houses and bridges with their superhuman strength. ... The trees in the temple and shrine grounds and the trees adorning rich men's gardens all groaned and shrieked at the highest pitch. Soon the earth's hair stood on end, and willows collapsed while bamboo stalks cracked.... One million people in all eight-hundred-and-eight blocks of Edo turned deathly pale, cowering in abject terror.

A more crucial factor accounting for the popularity of "The Five-storied Pagoda" is that it is a work perfect in its own way: Rohan's idealistic tendencies and literary skill matured to the extent that Jūbei is unmistakably a personification of Rohan's ideals—dedication to art and confidence in man's ability—yet at the same time quite believable as a simple carpenter with a personality of his own. This story manifests all the characteristics that distinguish Rohan's works in general, as Seki Ryōichi enumerates them: (1) the author's strong desire to express himself through protagonists; (2) artist-artisan heroes (especially in early phases); (3) disregard of, or aloofness from, mundane conventions; (4) mystic and allegorical tendencies; (5) propensity toward traditionalism; and (6) denouement through the use of *deus ex machina* (such as the Abbot Rōen) evoked by the sheer force of a protagonist's desperate determination and willpower.[5]

"The Five-storied Pagoda" has no superfluous characters, for even foil characters are well-developed and memorably individual. The primary emphasis is focused on characterization rather than effective verisimilitude, yet the emotional impact is heightened by realistic descriptions and dramatic scenes, leading in a crescendo to the final climax of the storm.

Jūbei finally lost his reserve and shouted in a loud voice that would reach even the main hall. "I beg for admission!" "You damned fool!" shouted back Tameemon even louder, reappearing promptly. "Men, throw this madman out!" The servants who had been loafing about in their quarters pounced on Jūbei, who planted himself firmly on the dirt floor to resist. "Hold his arms!" "Pull his feet!" The men were cursing and shrieking. . . .

"What is all this commotion?" At the Abbot's authoritative voice, the servants froze on the spot. Some were caught with their fists swung up midair, looking like Zen monks petrified by the opponent's shout in the middle of a heated Zen dialogue. Others hastened to hide behind one another tugging at their rolled-up sleeves in embarrassment. Tameemon, who had been at the height of haughty wrath almost billowing flames out of his flared nostrils, must have felt somewhat ashamed, but there was no escape for him, the ringleader. Drooping his head and rubbing both hands, he began to explain the situation, coloring the story to his own advantage. (Jūbei's first visit to Kannō Temple, Chapter 5–6)

Genta generously offered the building plans bearing his own cherished dream. Jūbei did not fail to appreciate Genta's genuine gallantry; yet he was also a man of integrity, and as such he refused to benefit from another man's resources. . . . Jūbei declined in words which sounded more curt than he intended. . . . Sharp-tempered Genta was no longer able to contain himself. . . . "Are you afraid that I might demand gratitude for these documents? Or else are you already so conceited as to dismiss my plans as altogether worthless? What a tactless fellow you are! It would have been a sensible thing for you to accept them with words of thanks, make use of a few plans, and acknowledge their merit afterward. But without so much as examining the bundle, you spurn them sight unseen as if their worthlessness were a matter of fact. . . . Beware of my watchful eyes lurking behind you. If it takes three years or even ten, I'll wait patiently for the day when I can pay you back in full."

Being of different temperaments, their wills clashed once, twice, and finally irreconcilably for the third time. "Mr. Jūbei," Genta lowered his voice, abruptly shifting to an overly polite speech. "I had better withdraw the rejected plans. No doubt you will build a fine pagoda by yourself, but I hope it will not fall apart in the first earthquake or storm." His lightly-delivered yet deeply scornful message was by no means pleasant to Jūbei. "Even this Slow-wit has a sense of honor," he blurted out, as if driving in the wedge of confidence. "I shall endeavor never to forget it," Genta delivered his warning, glowering fiercely at Jūbei without further words. (Confrontation at a restaurant, Chapter 22)

Jūbei was totally absorbed in drawing a relief design for a young helper, when Seikichi appeared, flying faster than a wild boar kicking up dust. His frenzied face flame-red and his bulging eyes fiercely upcast, he uttered a loud cry, "Damn you, Slow-wit! Drop dead!" Just as Jūbei turned on his heel in astonishment, Seikichi swung a razor-sharp adz set in a handle straight down with enough force to split a rock. An adz is as good as a sword in a carpenter's hand, and Jūbei was too late to dodge the blow and unable to withstand the impact. His left ear was sliced off and his shoulder was cut open. Seikichi lunged again. In flinging himself backward, Jūbei stepped into a toolbox, driving a five-inch nail right through his foot. Not missing his chance, Seikichi raised his adz, the tip of which reflected the setting sun to flash an artificial lightning. No sooner had it flashed than there arose a tiger's roar from behind Seikichi. "You fool!" shouted a man as he felled Seikichi with an easy sweep of a twelve-foot-long piece of lumber, tripping up his weak legs. (Chapter 25)

It is small wonder that "The Five-storied Pagoda" should have been the only one of Rohan stories that sold well. The Iwanami Bunko edition counted forty-five printings by 1963, selling over three-hundred-thousand copies in thirty-some years.

Except for four other works of fiction ("Love Bodhisattva," "A Sword," "A Saké Cup," and "Destiny") which had over ten editions, all his other works came out only in one or two editions.[6] But that is not to say that Rohan was little read. On the contrary, his name quickly acquired such prestige that no anthology of modern literature was conceivable without including his works, and literary magazines and intellectual monthlies competed in carrying articles by Rohan even after he began to write only nonfiction and scholarly treatises.

Rohan was totally disinterested in monetary gains for himself. For example, he continually refused to accept royalties from his 1913 play, *Nawa Nagatoshi* (about a fourteenth-century warrior lord of that name), on the ground that he had written it as a gift to celebrate the seventy-seventh birthday of the Baron Ōkura Kihachirō (of the Ōkura financial combine, 1837–1928). Yet it was performed on as many as ten occasions, the only one of his plays to be staged in his lifetime.[7] If necessary, nevertheless, he was capable of earning an impressive income from his writing, as he proved during his consumptive son's final hospitalization from June, 1925, to his death in November, 1926.[8]

Rohan is generally believed to have been less popular than Ozaki Kōyō, and for that matter, most other writers famous in their time. As far as his first phase is concerned, such a belief is unfounded. A magazine called *Edo Murasaki* (published by the Kenyūsha group, June, 1890, to December, 1891) ran a reader popularity poll in its first issue. The results reported on the July 25, 1890 issue were rather unexpected: Yamada Bimyō (a Kenyūsha deserter, so to speak), Kōyō, and Rohan led the list with eighty points each; Shōyō, sixty points; Mori Ōgai and the early romanticist Saganoya Omuro, forty each; and Futabatei Shimei, among others received only thirty points.[9] This magazine probably commanded a relatively sophisticated and literate readership, but it is still curious to note in retrospect that Rohan was favored over Futabatei. (Ōgai's score must reflect the impact of his literary criticism and translation of Western poetry, for his first work of fiction, "The Dancing Girl," appeared only five months before this poll.) Although Rohan was already acclaimed as the champion of "The Idealistic School" of literature with philosophical depth and insight, he was, in his twenties, also capable of assimilating entertaining plots and poetic beauty with serious ideals both transcendental and passionate.

Of comparative interest is a 1969 poll conducted by an academic journal, *Kokubungaku Kaishaku to Kanshō* (*Interpretation and Appreciation of Japanese Literature*) in January 1969. Forty-seven college professors and literary critics were asked to name, in order of preference, five Meiji writers they most admired. The following figures indicate the number of times each writer's name was mentioned: Natsume Sōseki—forty-two (twelve in first place); Mori Ōgai—thirty-five (six); Rohan—twenty-three (four); Shimazaki Tōson—nineteen (one); Futabatei Shimei—seventeen (none); and the rest included Kōyō and Shōyō, nine each. Rohan's surprisingly strong showing reflects his durable appeal to intellectual readers, even though the general public of today has long lost the ability to read Rohan's classical style.

CHAPTER 6

The Bodhisattva-errant Hero

I The Meiji Individualism

INVOLVED in "The Five-storied Pagoda" are a number of critical issues. First of all, Jūbei can be considered a champion of new Meiji individualism, which encouraged lofty aspiration beyond the confines of a traditional class system. By 1891, Japan's modernization was in full swing, accompanied by an inevitable social state of "the survival of the fittest" and individual rivalry to supersede the earlier, unified national effort and cooperation. On the one hand, Jūbei is a personification of egoism and exclusiveness innate in artists and modern technicians. The pagoda, in this sense, is a symbolic expression of the Meiji aspiration. At the same time, Jūbei is also a modern hero with the unswerving conviction, "All or nothing." Rohan eagerly read Plutarch's *Parallel Lives* and Carlyle's *On Heroes* and *The French Revolution*; he wrote detailed headnotes and annotations for Takahashi Gorō's translations of *Parallel Lives* (1925) and *The French Revolution* (1926). Rohan's idealistic characters echo heroism such as found in the lives of great historical figures whose human frailties and idiosyncrasies seem to intensify the significance of their achievements.

It was Rohan's belief that "man by nature must have an ambition or an ideal, for ambition is what separates man from animals" (XV, 249). Moreover, "ambition must be of the grandest magnitude and of the most sublime order" (XV, 247). "A man cannot expect to control his desires, resist temptations, correct himself, or take command of his mind, if his ambition is too meager or weak; and for this reason, Wang Yang-ming taught his disciples to aspire to sagehood. Man should set his aim at the apex" (XV, 251). The ideal or the ambition of the Confucian *kunshi* (scholar-gentleman) was to become a sage—

a man who has perfected himself morally and spiritually to be harmonious with the absolute. The Confucian gentleman was by no means an idle intellectual dilettante, for his ambition was inseparably conjoined to the betterment of society as a whole. The *kunshi* could bring salvation to society by acquiring virtues that were believed to be self-propagating. Successful realization of his ambition, therefore, hinged upon self-perfection, which involved two processes: moral discipline and intellectual activities.

Rohan wrote three commentaries on the *Analects*, one each during the Meiji, Taisho, and Showa periods. In the first of them, "Commentary on 'Government'" (1910), he describes the *kunshi* as a well-rounded, versatile man in contrast to a mediocrity who is limited to a certain fixed function (just as a small saké cup cannot serve as a soup bowl). And in "Joy and Pleasure" (1915), Rohan contends that a *kunshi*, with his multiple talents, is by no means a simple jack of all trades; as even a great writer cannot boast of unwritten masterpieces, a man is not a *kunshi* unless he employs his talents for the purpose of serving society. Such an idea may sound peculiar to today's readers, but Rohan's ultimate ambition was well understood by his contemporaries, as attested by the poet Kitamura Tōkoku (1868–1894), who in 1892 exclaimed: "It is my ardent wish that, rather than trying to imitate realist writers, a poet of ideals such as Rohan foster his imagination and perfect his philosophy of idealism so as to enlighten us, the ignorant mass."[1]

Rohan was, of course, aware that ambition could not be uniform or identical for all men. In "Mediocre Men and Superior Individuals," he suggests that every person according to his caliber aspire to accomplish the highest goal in his own field to contribute to the entire society. Once he was asked why he often chose artists and artisans for his heroes. He replied that loath to produce superfluous characters, he had tried to depict people "who would be able to function outside of the artificial world of fiction as well. They happened to emerge as the artist-artisan type, but it was simply a consequence of my determination to draw on real people, that is, people with real work to perform."[2] As the Rohanesque heroes pursue their goal with such intense passion and by all possible means, they stand in marked contrast to the superfluous heroes—the basically skeptical, unproductive protagonists dominating modern Japanese literature (such as Bunzō in *Ukigumo*, Kōyō's courtesans, Shimamura in Kawabata Yasunari's *Snow Country*, or even Sōseki's dilettante).

The nature of the artist's work—to create something new—has a great deal to do with Rohan's choice. The Confucians, especially during the Ming period, saw the fundamental characteristic of the universe (or the Way) as creativity or productivity, and they considered man as similarly creative in his very essence.[3] Wang Yang-ming's idea of sagehood was, moreover, "to stop relying on external standards, to become completely identical with the principle of nature (or Heaven) within oneself and thus become self-sustaining."[4] An artist can, as Rohan saw it, become a sage by creating a self-contained organic work of art. Without waiting for the introduction of the organic theory of art from the West, Rohan established his own organic view based on Oriental philosophies.

In the social context of the early Meiji, moreover, "ambition" was a prominent word: the most widespread form of ambition was typified by the slogan *risshin shusse* ("advance yourself socially"), which was applied to national purposes and needs as much as to individual aspiration.[5] The literary historian Itō Sei (1906–1969) notes that Rohan's artisan stories illustrate a poetic aspect of *risshin shusse shugi* ("social successism") in the Meiji period. He points out that until about 1900, aspiration for social success was still parallel and compatible with idealism; for, during the early stages of modernization, one was directly contributing to society by becoming a success in one's own field.[6]

More concretely, Rohan's positive hero portrays an image of a new Japanese youth envisioned by the leaders of the national essence movement during the Meiji twenties. They severely denounced what they called the "sneering youth," who emerged with the disillusioning decline of the people's rights movement; and the "kowtowing youth," who conformed to the system by selling their souls to social successism. As their antitheses, Tokutomi Sohō extolled the industrious youth (*rikisa-*

kugata seinen); and Miyake Setsurei called for the "Japanese of truth, goodness, and beauty" (*shinzenbi Nihon-jin*).[7] Rohan's artists embody the aesthetic beauty of Japanese tradition and the new positive youth driven by a sense of mission.

The new youth must be assiduous in his work and adventurous in his spirit. Adventure, says Rohan, is "not a reckless, senseless action nor an ignoble attitude expecting a lucky chance..., but it simply means to be unafraid of danger or difficulty in one's pursuit of the sublime goal" (XXIV, 328). In fact, the will to suffer in creation is essential in an artist's life. "I shall undertake painstaking endeavor in my writing career," declares Rohan, "for I would be infinitely ashamed to spend my life shunning hardships" (XXIV, 189). Creation is a lonely struggle, for an artist has only his own individuality and uncompromising conviction to rely on. At a meeting of Seinen Bungaku Kai (Literary Association of Young Men, a youth branch of the romantic Bungakukai group) in 1891, Rohan made a speech entitled "Conquest of Bookcases." He warned the aspiring young writers that no great literature would be born until a writer freed himself from bookcases (past literature) and nurtured his own creativity. He advocated that a writer or a poet build bookcases of his own to overshadow the past literature and to produce works long-lasting and universal, that is, true to human nature rather than to himself alone.

In an article on Saikaku, to quote one of Rohan's most famous passages, he cries out, "Born in the glorious era of Meiji, why should I worship the dried residue of the past masters?" (XV, 9). Similarly, he asserts in another discourse, "Of course, we must respect history, which none of us have the right to wantonly destroy. At the same time, we are children of history, not its slaves" (XV, 281). In pursuit of freedom from the limitations and expectations of contemporary society, Rohan admired Takizawa Bakin (1767–1848; the master writer of late Edo didactic historical romances) for his ethical stand that was shared by Rohan himself: "Bakin's life cut a horizontal line across his own time, while other writers lived parallel to their times. Not a man to drift along with the fashions of his period, he passed critical judgment on his era, applying a set of intransigent criteria" (XV, 311). Man must establish his ideal, asserts Rohan, to use it as though it were a rigid ruler made of steel, not of rubber, if he expects to maintain independence of mind and accurate judgment: everything must be measured by such a ruler and corrected accordingly. Hence the principle of "all or nothing" by which Jūbei refuses compromise of any sort.

II Art Glorified

The second motif in "The Five-storied Pagoda" is the immortality of art. Jūbei represents romantic aestheticism, which had been gathering momentum in Japan since around 1887,[8] to be stimulated all the more by the works of the English Pre-Raphaelites (especially Dante Gabriel Rossetti) and the critical theories of Walter Pater, the spokesman for the art-for-art's-sake movement. Rossetti's name was mentioned for the first time in Japan by Mori Ōgai in a phrase "Rossetti's neo-romantic poetry" (Ima no Igirisu Bungaku, March, 1890). A more detailed introduction came much later in December, 1893, when Waseda Bungaku carried an article based on W. Basil Worsfold's critical review of Rossetti found in the British journal, Nineteenth Century (renamed Twentieth Century).[9]

Preceding it by two years, Rohan had independently achieved in "The Five-storied Pagoda" the Pre-Raphaelite ideal of "combining realistic fidelity in detail with a romantic mysticism in the general effect."[10] Rossetti's influence blossomed later in the poetry of the full-fledged Japanese romanticists (Nihon Rōman-ha, for example, Shimazaki Tōson, 1872–1943; and Yosano Akiko, 1878–1942) but chiefly in sensuous beauty and vague symbolism. Even before Walter Pater became fashionable in Japan, Rohan had written a work embodying one of the general ideals of both classical and romantic schools of the West, such as reaffirmed by Pater: "the organic union of form and content, in which the end is not distinct from the means ... the subject from the expression."[11]

Nevertheless, Rohan was by no means a believer in the art-for-art's-sake idea. The raison d'être of art, as he saw it, must be identical with that of religion—aspire to Buddhahood and enlighten mankind; for art can inspire and educate man, show visions of perfection, and convey the knowledge of the absolute. Art as artificial creation serves as *hōben* (*upaya* or "means") by which man can be led to the ultimate knowledge. A poem in the *Vimalakīrti Sūtra* declares that *pāramitā* ("wisdom") is the mother of all bodhisattvas, and *upaya* ("means") their father.[12] (*Upaya* is believed to require intellect, supposedly a male virtue.)

The *Lotus Sutra* (in which "Hōbenbon," or the *Upaya* Chapter, teaches the usefulness of expedient devices such as "*jūnyoze*, ten such-likenesses" in explaining the universe) compares the Buddha's love to a father's love for his sons, as illustrated in the Parable of the Burning House. Japanese artists were traditionally regarded as heirs to their masters either by blood or by superior skill. It is not for a sentimental effect that Rohan describes the episode of Jūbei's young son building an imitation pagoda. The boy is an acolyte learning the sacred art to become a future bodhisattva-errant.

In Rohan's view, art discriminates against no one, for creativity is man's very nature; and artistic accomplishment is the most sublime of all human achievements. Through it, man can compete with nature and may even be able to win. Jūbei's pagoda is a testimony to the beauty and sublimity of art as a crystallization of man's spiritual essence. The storm that threatens and tests the pagoda signifies, at the same time, the contest between man and Nature. Only when Jūbei and Genta together stand by the pagoda representing mankind, in order to protect man's creation, does Nature concede defeat. (This is clearly indicated by the Abbot's final inscription.)

At the same time, the storm also mirrors the psychological conflict between Genta and Jūbei generated by idiosyncratic dissimilarities; but it is not petty personal antagonism. While Jūbei is undoubtedly his ideal hero, Rohan is simultaneously identifying with Genta. Halfway through the writing of "The Five-storied Pagoda," Rohan himself circled the Tennō Temple pagoda in a fierce storm fearing for its safety, and he incorporated this experience into the storm scene. Furthermore, Rohan's own "Dictionary of Current Personal Names" (1900) discloses that "Genta" meant "lumber" in the dialect of Owari (present-day Nagoya).

Genta as a man of lumber can be considered a representative

of all carpenter-architects. The storm, then, signifies the relent-lessly critical appraisal by nature and by fellow artist-artisans to which a work of art is subjected, as well as mankind's desperate and concerted effort to preserve one possible proof of man's spiritual immortality. The pagoda is a symbol of man's supreme challenge to nature and impermanence.

Art as artificial creation may even be superior to nature in its power to enlighten man. "Viewing of a Painting" (1925) deals with the case of a student of mature age nicknamed Taiki Bansei Sensei (Master Late Bloomer). After many years of hard work and saving, Bansei finally enters college but soon suffers from a neurosis. On a journey to nurse his mind back to health, he spends a night in a bleak temple in the gloomy mountains during a fierce rain storm. Suddenly he realizes that all the sounds in the world, past and present, are contained in the sound of falling rain: in the single steady tone, "zaaaa," he can distinguish the train whistle, cattle mooing, children singing, people laughing, quarreling, rejoicing—all the sounds audible to man. Muttering to himself, "Oh, well," he falls asleep.

Awakened later, he is led to a hut higher on the mountain to escape the encroaching flood. Almost covering one wall of the small room is a large painting of a magnificent city by a beautiful river, with mountains, houses, valleys, boats, and people going about their business peacefully. As he attentively examines the picture, he sees and actually hears a ferryman open his mouth wide and announce, "Last call!" Just as Bansei is about to answer, "I'm coming!," a draft of cold air causes the light to flicker, and the ferry and the ferryman recede into two dimensions. "It was just one moment, without beginning or end" (V, 408). Bansei's neurosis is cured, and he is said to have become a farmer. "Whether the great talent failed to bloom at all or he had already bloomed, it probably no longer mattered to Bansei" (V, 409), concludes Rohan.

Hearing the sound of the rain, Bansei is able to attain a partial enlightenment, merely enough to ascend one more level (higher on the mountain); but through contemplation of the picture (as in religious training), he reaches the ultimate state where the distinction between reality and illusion (art) ceases to exist. The life in the painting is actually his life, for he has come to live in "a moment without beginning or end," that is, the eternal present. What art can create is not a static, conceptual plane but a dynamic moment embracing time, space, self, others, existence, emptiness—all opposites and antitheses.[13] It is significant that Bansei acquires the knowledge of this eternal moment by entering into a painting, which by nature exists in eternal time. Art is greater not only because it outlives man, as John Keats noted with envy, but also, and more intrinsically, because it is a cosmic entity existing in the eternal moment for Rohan. Whereas Keats's Grecian urn is a "foster-child of silence and slow time," Rohan's painting is the eternal, omnipresent, vital, eloquent cosmos in itself, for by the principle of undifferentiation of all things, every moment is identical with eternity.

III   *Faith in Man*

Such inexorable belief in the power of art (man's creation) is naturally accompanied by an equally limitless confidence in man. The third issue presented in "The Five-storied Pagoda" is humanism. The supreme Buddhist goal is revealed in the bodhisattva concept of Mahayana philosophy. It is the postulate without which life has no meaning for a Buddhist; it is both man's innate wish (*gan*) to be delivered from the miseries of existence and the Buddha's Original Vow (*hongan*) to save mankind. The bodhisattva concept is summed up in the familiar words, *jōgubodai gekeshujō* ("aspire to Buddhahood and enlighten mankind").

The term bodhisattva has multilevel meanings. In early Buddhism, it referred to Gautama Buddha in his former lives as a "being of enlightenment" (*bodhi-sattva*) in the sense that he was destined for enlightenment. Historically this term designated laymen who tended the stupa in which the Buddha's remains were enshrined: they were "seekers of enlightenment," for they worshipped the stupa as the embodiment of the Buddha himself. On the metaphysical level, the bodhisattva is viewed as having attained a stage of enlightenment surpassed only by Buddhahood. One can become a bodhisattva through bodhisattva practices, such as genuine love of mankind, endurance of all persecutions, and attainment of the knowledge that all things are

empty.[14] Finally on the most familiar, but not the least significant, level, the bodhisattva is revered as one who has attained
enlightenment but chooses to postpone his entry into Nirvana
until all sentient beings on earth have been saved. It is in
this sense of the potential Buddha who denies himself Nirvana
in order to help man save himself that the bodhisattva concept
has made the greatest impact on the Japanese mind.

Illustrated in the famous Parable of the Burning House in
the *Lotus Sutra* is the idea of *gan*—man's innate *wish* to be
saved, and the bodhisattva's *vow* to help man. A *chōja* (elder
who is wealthy as much in virtue and wisdom as in material
riches) returns home to find his house on fire with his three
sons inside, unaware of the danger. The father urges them to
come out of the burning house, but they are too preoccupied
with their game to heed his advice. The father coaxes them out
by promising to give them treasure carts drawn by a sheep,
a deer, or an ox. Once outside, each of the sons receives, instead
of three different lesser carts as promised, a white-ox cart
laden with precious gifts.[15]

This parable teaches the principle of the Great Vehicle, by
which the universal salvation of Mahayana is achieved, in
contrast to Hinayana beliefs in hierarchically selective, limited
salvation by the Three Small Vehicles. (The Shrāvaka vehicle
for the direct disciples of the Buddha; the Pratyeka-Buddha
vehicle for those pursuing enlightenment on their own without
a master; and the Bodhisattva vehicle.)[16] At the same time, it
is a story illustrating the bodhisattva's love for man and his
means of guidance that is sometimes expedient but always
justified by the purpose: the father (bodhisattva) saves his son
(man) by luring him out of a burning house (complacent life)
with the reward of treasures (truth). Man must wish to be
saved before it is possible for the bodhisattva to save him. The
Abbot's tale in "The Five-storied Pagoda" is Rohan's version of
this parable. Only if man learns the futility of selfishness will
a pebble appear identical with a jewel, and will he realize that
all things are the same in essence. Rohan's version emphasizes
universal salvation through the selfless, unified efforts of mankind.

For Rohan, the bodhisattva concept was a feasible ideal, by
no means merely a philosophical abstraction. In the person of

Ninomiya Sontoku (1787–1856), for example, Rohan found
substantiation of the bodhisattva vow and wrote his biography
(1891) for the inspiration of young readers. (Sontoku was a
true Confucian scholar-gentleman who aided farmers by providing technical advice on such matters as agricultural improve-
ment and reclamation of land as well as spiritual guidance. He
stressed the virtue of labor, planned agrarian economy in a
communal order, and a view of life as a continuing act of
thanksgiving for the Heaven, earth, and man.)[17]

Rohan further asserted that a writer, being an artist, cannot
by nature help but aspire to be a bodhisattva. He expressed
his admiration for Bakin's "great talent, remarkable energy, and
artistic view fused with his staunch sense of justice—his fierce
artistic conscience with which he worked for scores of years
on the principle of 'reward the good and chastise the evil'"
(XV, 302). In Rohan's "Evil Wind in the Chaotic World" (1890),
a beautiful woman sends a letter of indictment to the attorney
general of a fictitious country, deploring the moral confusion
of the people. She denounces scholars for not educating the
people, politicians for being indifferent to widespread moral
chaos, priests for not being virtuous enough to lead the people.
But above all, she reproaches writers for their superficiality and
myopic vision, because they "ought to be the light illuminating
the world inside and out for eternity and ought to raise their
sight beyond one generation and one country" (I, 493).

The artist charged with the mission to lead the people, demands Rohan, must perfect himself first so he may save others.
The long arduous process of self-perfection is often expressed
in literature by the metaphor of a journey. In his second story,
"Love Bodhisattva," Rohan sets his sculptor hero on a journey
to seek inspiration from great works of art. The journey is a
traditional means of religious and artistic training that figured
large in the lives of great poets such as Bashō and Saigyō, whom
Rohan loved. But at the same time, it also suggests a gradual
yet dramatic approach toward the secrets of art, religion, or
the universe itself. "Love Bodhisattva" begins with a section
entitled *nyozegamon* ("So I have heard"). For the heading
of the ten succeeding chapters, Rohan borrowed from the *Lotus
Sutra* a philosophical concept known as *jūnyoze* ("ten such-

likenesses," or ten categories of supreme truth as manifested in mundane experience, that is, ten relative truths). The story ends with the twelfth section called *shohō jissō* (all *dharma* reflects the true state). Shu'un's journey is, therefore, the spiritual ascent of a man's soul seeking knowledge and self-perfection.

A man confident in advancing such a view must be a humanist who loves and applauds man as well as a romantic optimist who believes in the ultimate perfectibility of man and society. This point did not escape Rohan's contemporaries, who classified Rohan, together with Mori Ōgai, as a rare Apollonian type in contrast to the numerous Dionysian types who fill the pages of Japanese literary history. The Apollonian type (at least in the Japanese sense) is identified with intellect rather than instinct, and in Rohan's case, also approbation and healthy adoration of life, and a humanistic glorification of man.

Rohan's apotheosis of man arises from an affirmative, optimistic view of man as possessing an innate ideal nature that corresponds to religious and moral ideals. Rohan is in this regard an orthodox Confucian who sees human nature as basically good. Confucianism dealt quite exclusively with man's life in this world here and now, aspiring to improve and perfect society and man. Humanism is the basic tenet of Confucianism, the central concept of which is *jen* ("humanity"), the universal common nature in man. Moreover, even a Neo-Taoist book, *Pao-p'u Tzu*, affirms that man has an innate wisdom by the power of which he can perceive cosmic mysteries and attain immortality.[18] Within the Japanese tradition, the concept of *makoto* ("sincerity," "fidelity to genuine emotion") predominating the *Man'yōshū* (an eighth-century anthology of poetry) derives also from the belief that a spontaneous expression of the human heart would reflect the unadulterated, therefore ideal, state of human nature.

True insight, or the ultimate wisdom, in Buddhist terms is called *prajñā*, which the Heart Sutra equates with great compassion. Man can attain self-perfection by means of *prajñā*, affirms Mahayana Buddhism, because all things (animate and inanimate) possess the Buddha Nature in them. The Bodhisattva Kannon is conceived as the symbol of mercy who appears in the guise of any being that serves best to save a particular person in a particular situation. This concept metaphorically embraces the reverse truth that every being possesses the potential to become a Kannon. The *Lotus Sutra* tells an episode of a man named Sadâparibhūta, who bowed to everyone, saying, "I do not slight you, for you are all future Buddhas."[19] He eventually became the Slight-No-One Bodhisattva through such awareness of the universal Buddha Nature and determined observance of bodhisattva practices, the most important of which is veneration of man. One must revere man, believed Rohan, because every man is a potential Buddha worthy of veneration; and a man is sinful only when his Buddha Nature is clouded or obstructed by desires and weaknesses. That is why even the murder of Hikoemon the whaler is expiated through dedicated labor, and the villainous uncle in "Love Bodhisattva" repents in the end and follows his niece-turned-bodhisattva to heaven.

Rohan advocates self-help or man's will to save himself by performing good deeds, by doing penance, or even by making the effort simply to say prayers; for no man is beyond salvation and Buddhist love is all-inclusive. In a sense, Rohan's egalitarian view reflected the mood of early Meiji society, in which all four classes (samurai, farmers, artisans, and merchants) were declared equal by the Constitution. It is owing to Rohan's humanistic belief in the social equality of all people that Tae in "Encounter With a Skull" can reject the love of a nobleman, and Jūbei is allowed to bid for a job against his master.

Based on a story in *Shuryōgon-gyō* (*Sūramgama Sutra*), Rohan wrote "Purakurichi" (1932). An Indian girl named Prakritī falls in love with Ananda, a handsome disciple of Gautama Buddha, after Ananda unhesitatingly drank water handed out by her, an untouchable. In her agonies of mad longing, she appeals to the Buddha to grant her love, whereupon the Buddha dispels her illusion of love by teaching the emptiness of the flesh. She becomes a nun, and the religious community is scandalized by the entry of an untouchable among their ranks. Thereupon, the Buddha expounds the truth of the equality of all castes by revealing the former existences of all concerned.

Rohan's faith in man's capability did not lead to egocentric individualism. Jūbei's desire to build the pagoda is motivated by the artist's instinct for self-expression and his urge to create a perfect work of art. He is, moreover, ordered to build it by a mysterious figure who appears in his dream. While Genta is concerned with the judgment of posterity, Jūbei is pitting himself against the destructive forces of nature and the ultimate perfection personified by the Demon King and the Abbot Rōen. It is not by an arbitrary choice that Rohan pictured the storm as an assault of the host of demons rather than as natural forces of wind and rain, and the sea storm in *The Whaler* as apparitions of Hikoemon's slain victims haunting him. In most religions, divine beings are visualized in human form. Rohan presents the forces of retribution also in human form, whether ghost, devil, woman, or apparition. Rohan the poet was able to humanize and personify the abstract ideals conceived by Rohan the philosopher. And Rohan the writer had only one subject matter—mankind, unlike most Japanese writers who were only concerned with their own limited personal worlds.

In "The Blood-red Star" (1891), a mad poet called Kaihi (All Negative) is invited to the moon palace. Arrogantly expecting heavenly applause, he asks for a subject on which to compose a poem. The exquisite moon princess says, "Here on the moon, the only object of our love and worship is man. We would like you to compose on the subject of Man. If it is too broad, please narrow it down to Mr. Kaihi, yourself."

Instantly, his brain boiled, heart burst, liver split; his chest froze in the ice of awe, entrails singed in the fire of remorse; half his muscles were limp from despondence, the other half twitching in rage; hot blood sprayed out of his pores, and black smoke billowed through his gnashing teeth. His eyes blazing and his body engulfed in flames, he uttered a piercing scream. Then, he plunged, a blood-red star, hurtling headlong through the infinite space. (II, 90)

The poet Kaihi's entire existence was annihilated the moment he realized that he had failed to understand himself, not to mention mankind. A failure to depict the real man is, at least in Rohan's view, a fatal flaw in literature, the *raison d'être* of which is to help man understand his own true nature and attain enlightenment.

It is in an attempt to delineate the divine aspect of human nature that Rohan humanizes and personifies divine beings while deifying and mythicizing human beings. Tae in "Encounter With a Skull" is a Benzai Tennyo (Heavenly Maiden Benzai), who is usually depicted in Buddhist and secular art as a beautiful girl dressed in grass robes living in a humble mountain hut far from the madding world.[20] The heroine of "Venomous Coral Lips" in a mountain retreat is in love with the Buddha, for he has written the sutras, the most beautiful poems in the world. (This is not a sacrilegious concept but rather reminiscent of Christian nuns' ritual marriage to Christ.) The Buddha is a poet moved by the pathos of things (*mono no aware*), and sutras are all poems expressing his love for mankind; the Buddha and sutras are all the more sacred for that reason. In Rohan's eyes, the one who is best able to save mankind is the poet. Then, who else is the greatest of the poets if not the Buddha?

Rohan, however, was far from being a shallow-minded optimist. He was aware that reality was not quite so tractable in the face of ideals. The liberated man must still fight and often taste defeat in reality, and his defeat may be all the more tragic for his self-awareness. It was necessary, therefore, not only to point out the evils and vices to guide people away from indulgence, but most positively, to show the glimpses of hope and the world attainable beyond reality. Rohan's best works are his attempts to picture such ideal worlds as an incentive to encourage the aspiration toward self-enlightenment. There are two methods of achieving enlightenment. Man can reinforce and enlarge his individuality by means of willpower and innate ability till his own self coincides in part with the universal, ideal Self: Rohan's artist heroes improve their fate through dedication to their arts and eventually attain the ideal. The alternative is the conquest and elimination of man's self so as to submerge into the universal Self: it is by such sublimation of the superficial identity that Tae, after her body has been consumed by leprosy, arrives at the realm of perfect composure to be related to all times and all souls.

IV *Religious Symbolism*

Eternity and cosmic vision constitute the fourth issue in "The Five-storied Pagoda"—the religious symbolism. On this

level, Jūbei takes on a role comparable to that of a savior: he
builds a perfect object of religious worship believed to be
endowed with the power to purify and enlighten recreant mankind; and it is he who courageously confronts the legion of
demons while apostate people cower and panic. Romantic
mysticism is exalted to a sublime plane until man is placed in
a supernatural cosmic realm with superhuman beings in this
story. Many a Japanese critic has been reminded, especially
by the storm scene, of Milton's *Paradise Lost*. In 1906, Rohan
named five great literary figures who had influenced him most:
"Shakespeare, Milton, Goethe, Ssu-ma Ch'ien, and Tu Fu"
(XL, 693). Milton's name was first mentioned as early as in
1853 (*Igirisu Kiryaku*, or *An Outline of English History*) and
1861 (*Eikokushi*, or *History of England*). Nevertheless, exactly
when Rohan read *Paradise Lost* has yet to be determined.
"The Five-storied Pagoda" itself proves its Buddhist origin:
the demons are not rebels against God but rather beings who
come to protect the Law and punish the arrogant; and above
the moral chaos and human struggle, there is a realm of peace,
harmony, and wisdom attainable by man, as exemplified in the
person of the Abbot (whose name means "Radiant Sphere").

Eternity and cosmos are symbolized by a stupa in the *Lotus
Sutra*. When an ancient Buddha called the Abundant Treasure
Buddha finished his course and approached the entry into
Nirvana, he instructed, "After my extinction, those who desire
to worship my whole body should erect a great Stupa," and
he vowed, "If in any country in the universe there be a place
where the Lotus Flower Sutra is preached, let my Stupa arise
and appear there, in order that I may harken to that Sutra,
bear testimony to it, and extol it."[21] In a dramatic scene, a
magnificent vision of a stupa appears in midair over the crowd
witnessing the Abundant Treasure Buddha entering Nirvana.

Jūbei's pagoda is thus a symbol of the Buddha's whole body,
and its construction is a religious rite in itself. It takes absolute
concentration and negation of all other desires as well as a
concerted effort of all mankind. Only when the entire crew
works in unity (as after Jūbei's injury) can the pagoda escape
the fate of the Tower of Babel. The vision of the Stupa, moreover, is to appear exclusively on the occasion when the teaching

of the Lotus is being preached, testifying, "All is true that thou sayest."[22] Conversely, the building of a pagoda was traditionally believed to signify efficacious preaching of the *Lotus Sutra*. Viewed in this context, Jūbei's role takes on a sacerdotal significance, and the storm implies a divine test of Jūbei's true faith.

The symbolism of the stupa in the *Lotus Sutra* is by no means limited to the religious level. As Gautama Buddha is expounding the gospel of the White Lotus, a mystic stupa does indeed spring from the ground into the air. When its doors open, an emaciated figure of the Abundant Treasure Buddha is seen within. He moves over to one side and invites Gautama Buddha to sit next to him. The stupa in which the two Buddhas are seated side by side symbolizes the eternal cosmos, with the ancient Buddha and the present Buddha bearing testimony to the identity and unity of all times and all beings. The ending of "The Five-storied Pagoda" indicates that Rohan did in fact mirror this mystic, cosmic stupa in Jūbei's pagoda.

The present Buddha, from a curl of white hair in the middle of his forehead, sends forth a ray of light to project visions of all Buddhas and all Buddha Lands in the air. The Abundant Treasure Buddha, who is already extinct yet immanent, has become emaciated in proportion to the decline of faith in the world. As noted by an early translator of the *Lotus Sutra*, Hendrik Kern, the present Buddha is the symbol of the sun, and the ancient Buddha the moon.[23] Jūbei's pagoda, which is seen launching the moon and swallowing the sun, is undoubtedly the Abundant Treasure Stupa; and it is the universe, where man has the hope of salvation by the help of the merciful Buddhas who vowed to save mankind. It may even be Nirvana itself or the Western Paradise, whence the ancient Buddha returns to lead mankind and whither the present Buddha is headed after his extinction. (Rohan deliberately makes the moon rise from Jūbei's pagoda and the sun set into it, reversing the familiar imagery of the rising sun.) Art is thus magnified and elevated by Rohan to symbolize the hope, the purpose, and the essence of man's existence in the universe.

Rohan may be considered a didactic writer to the extent that his works usually convey some meaningful messages. Nonetheless, he was not a moralist in the strict sense. His heroes transcend the dictates of conventional moral codes without a trace of guilt feeling. Driven by an artistic aspiration that is not a take-it-or-leave-it playful pursuit but an intense and serious inner calling, Jūbei must transcend the customary heroics such as the typical Edoite generosity displayed by Genta or the human sentiments by which his wife lives. As Zen Buddhism teaches, "If you meet your parents, kill them. If you meet the Buddha, kill the Buddha as well,"[24] mundane human relationships and preconceived ideas only stand in one's way to enlightenment.

Shu'un rescues Tatsu and allows himself to be put in the position of her guardian out of chivalrous spirit, which demands an act without expectation of reward. But his own emotion (budding love for Tatsu) and outside pressure (Tatsu's father claiming her) interfere with his gallant action. He surmounts this crisis by immersing himself in artistic concentration. Rohan's ideal character is no doubt Jūbei, who typifies uncompromising commitment to art, absolute confidence in his own skill, total abnegation of unartistic aspects of life, and undeflectable passion for achievement. Tsubouchi Shōyō observed in 1892:

Rohan expressed the view that every man must preserve his own individuality, never allowing himself to be assimilated into anything to the point of losing it. He expounds the virtue and the benefit of individuality, asserting that it is the only means available for a man to save himself. I have not yet ascertained whether or not Ibsen's individualism is similar to Rohan's. But in stressing the individual will and in believing that the will is intensified and energized by each obstacle to be virtually omnipotent, Rohan does resemble Browning, who accords so much significance to the power of emotion.[25]

More specifically, some modern scholars detect certain parallels between Rohan's Jūbei and Ibsen's hero in the idealistic play *Brand* (1866), in their unmitigated passion, their total commitment, and their earnest response to the calling from the absolute.[26] They each build a religious monument to awaken morally complacent people, and both suffer persecution by society. As incarnate will itself, Jūbei is an embodiment of individualism, as is the clergyman Brand. Yet their dissimilarities are more revealing than their affinity. Brand's uncompromising demand for "All or Nothing" alienates him from everyone except his boy child (whose frail life is claimed by the cold climate) and his faithful wife (who dies of anguish), sacrificed to his mission; whereas Jūbei's votive offerings are an ear (severed by an irate colleague) and possibly his own life. Brand's is a lonely tragic struggle after he repudiates his new church as a temple of idolatry, but Jūbei is a divinely inspired artist-priest protecting the pagoda—a symbol of human willpower and the Buddha's body itself. Brand is destined to die alone in an avalanche, defeated by nature, while Jūbei triumphs over nature's test and succeeds in his mission.

Brand, facing death, asks God whether he has earned salvation by virtue of his dedication to the mission. A voice calls through the thunder of the snow and ice, "God is Love!"[27] As for this mystifying ending, there are three possible interpretations: first, he is being punished for his lack of love for fellowmen; second, he is granted salvation by the grace of God, who shows more compassion than Brand ever practiced; and the third answer is offered by Irving Deer, who emphasizes the theological explanation that Brand's uncertainty about the merit of his absolutism reveals his essential humanity and earns him salvation, for man is inherently doomed to failure precisely because he is a man and not God.[28]

Herein lies the fundamental distinction between the Christian martyr and Rohan's bodhisattva hero. An irrevocable chasm separating God and man nullifies any hope for man to become God. Brand can be called a tragic hero who failed due to character flaws (such as lack of human compassion) or his opposite—a villain afflicted with the supreme hubris of absolutism, as Brand was labeled by George Bernard Shaw in *The Quintessense of Ibsenism* (1891). Jūbei is decidedly not a tragic hero: aside from his final triumph, his seeming eccentricity and extremism are never meant to be tragic flaws; on the contrary, they are the very essence of Jūbei the man and indispensable qualities in a bodhisattva hero.

Before becoming a bodhisattva, Rohan believed, man must first become a nonhuman, a social outcast by conventional standards but a being with fewer human limitations. Ibsen's Brand, a Christian, may be saved because he is human in his self-doubt, but the Buddhist Jūbei must paradoxically transcend humanness in order to be truly humane. Astounded by Jūbei's adamant refusal to accept his master's offer of a joint project, his wife asks, "Without a doubt you will be ostracized as an ingrate, a social deviate, a beast without human feelings, a dog, a crow. What glory is there in undertaking a job if you must turn yourself into a dog or a crow?" Jūbei later confides in her: "Well, I just can't help myself. It is my very obstinacy that makes me what I am. It makes me Jūbei the Slow-wit." Not only is personal glory or satisfaction quite meaningless for a Rohanesque hero but he must transcend it that he may bring true glory to the world.

If Rohan's individualism resembles Ibsen's, then, it is only in the single-minded drive to respond to a calling at the risk of self-extinction as in *Brand,* but never in the hedonistic, self-indulgent pursuit of one's own desires typified by *Peer Gynt,* the better-known counterpart of *Brand.* Ibsen was introduced to Japan by Tsubouchi Shōyō in his article, "Hendrik Ibsen" (*Waseda Bungaku,* November, 1893). Rohan's "The Five-storied Pagoda" was serialized in the *Kokkai* Newspaper from November, 1892, to March, 1893. It is improbable that Rohan had been exposed to Ibsen's works before 1893.

Rohan's individualism is closer to the Ming Neo-Confucian concept of individuality. "Neo-Confucianism brings to recognition an evident but difficult truth, namely, that individuality in the human being will be unique, not alone in what he is, but in what he does. His life may be expected to yield something significant—not only different—and something which *no one else can do.* In this deed, the individual is realized."[29] Rohan's heroes are not only action-oriented but also self-confident and intrepid. From a Neo-Confucian point of view, "one's mental and moral capacities greatly depend on one's physical powers and drives for their development. Even the so-called [Buddhist] School of the Mind does not see the mind as a disembodied spirit but rather as a vital power manifested through the physical aspect of man, his material force or ether [*ch'i*]."[30]

Most of Rohan's heroes are depicted as powerfully built, tall, and masculine. Kiken the Rare Man, Kasai Dairoku the Bearded Man, and Hikoemon the harpooner are typical examples. Jūbei's name can also mean "a heavy man," and his nickname "Nossori" describes the rather slow movements of a massive man as well as slow-wittedness. Even Shōzō the swordsmith, after three years of utter concentration, still has an enormous figure. Not to be overlooked is Rohan's article, "On Great Men," in which Rohan illustrates metaphorically: a great man is a person who is not easily or quickly fulfilled and therefore continues to pursue a more distant, greater goal, just as the larger the bowl, the longer it takes to fill it. The titles of Rohan's works also add to the masculine, therefore dynamic, impression by their male imagery as well as their Freudian symbolism, in sword, star, towering pagoda, whaler, gun, statue, and the like.

His tendency toward masculinity, however, is not an expression of contempt for, or condemnation of, women. On the contrary, there are few other Japanese writers who endowed their female characters with more heroic spirit, humanistic cultivation, and insight than Rohan did Rubina of "Dewdrops," Tae of "Encounter With a Skull," the Madonna-Eve, mystic lady in "Enlightenment of Love," Rikyū's wife, and others. If his heroines seem to be equipped with typically male virtues, it is because such virtues are, in Rohan's eyes, the fundamental ideal qualities in any human being. In fact, Rohanesque heroines are as much bodhisattvas as their male counterparts.

While man is fighting against the evil in himself and in society toward the remote goal of enlightenment, he needs to be armed with an indomitable spirit and an unswerving ambition. Without them, man cannot survive hardships nor follow the rules in religious discipline. The way to immortality is so simple and easy, says *Pao-p'u Tzu*, that only lack of ambition and insufficient faith prevent a person from achieving it.[31] Buddhist enlightenment is impossible, nevertheless, without the knowledge that suffering is an inevitable part of life. And more crucially, enlightenment requires an acceptance of suffering. If the positive hero is inspired by a mission of mercy to save mankind, his pursuit of the goal must be resolute and relentless.

The definition of mercy or great compassion is not a simple

matter. *Hagakure*, the Nabeshima Clan house codes recorded around 1716, lists four sacrosanct pledges of the samurai: first, not to fail in the way of the warrior; second, to serve one's lord with good faith; third, to be pious toward one's parents; but the fourth is, rather unexpectedly, to practice great compassion to serve people.[32] It is not farfetched, accordingly, to see Rohan's samurai heroes as practicing the way of the bodhisattva as much as his artisan heroes. The bodhisattva helps man in the spirit of mercy but man can be led astray by false compassion as well. Whereas the Devil tried to tempt Christ in the wilderness with the visions of glory and power, the Buddha meditating under the bodhi tree was approached by a devil Namuci, who wept in false compassion urging the Buddha to terminate his agonizing contemplation and fast.[33] True compassion sometimes lies in denying the sufferer immediate relief or perhaps even in a combative attitude as Nichiren believed.

Jūbei's stubborn refusal to compromise is reminiscent of the most extreme and aggressive faction of Nichiren Sect known as the *Fujufuse-ha* (Receive-not—Offer-not faction). It originates with Nichiō (1565–1630), who urged his followers not to receive alms from, nor to give religious services for, nonbelievers of the *Lotus Sutra*. Nichiō saw this as the purest form of the bodhisattva way, refusing any type of compromise in his effort to turn Japan into the Buddha Land here and now.[34] Jūbei's obstinacy is true mercy in this sense, for in compromising he would jeopardize the fate of mankind. Rohan's heroes, nevertheless, have no conscious intention of becoming bodhisattvas. They suffer, struggle, endeavor, and eventually succeed, simply as human beings without an awareness of their symbolic role.

Rohan advises, "To value individuality does not entail rejection of others. Man must be like a well-ploughed field, soft and moist, ever ready to soak up light, heat, or cold. . . . A man without furrows of belief cannot be disciplined in his emotion" (XXV, 123). For the truly ambitious and the able, however, Rohan extols the "pleasure of independence": "It is the rebel of one age that heralds a new age; and it is the adversary of one era that formulates the thought of the next era. . . . Very few can endure the anguish and loneliness of independence to stand heroically alone, but history is invariably bejeweled with such men of independent mind" (XXVIII, 301).

When Rohan is successful, as in "The Five-storied Pagoda," his bodhisattva-errant hero personifies mankind in its sublime essence, and his work of art is a manifestation of man's immortal spirit—a supreme unity of passion, faith and intellect. At this point, man's creation, including literature, signifies at once man's confrontation with the absolute and the perfect, not to challenge their existence but to become part of them. Such union is possible, in Rohan's view, for a work of art into which man's entire being is submerged must naturally come to bear a mystical spiritual force. Thus, Rohan idealizes human power to a degree that it appears potent enough to render the impossible possible and his positive heroes emerge as bodhisattva-errants striving, if unwittingly, to fulfill the bodhisattva vow to enlighten mankind.

CHAPTER 7

The Mature Phase (1893–1896)

I The Minute Storehouse of Life

THE image of Rohan the crusading novelist in the idealistic phase is transformed into that of a more objective, tranquil philosopher in the second period. It starts with *The Minute Storehouse of Life*, his most expansive novel, serialized in the newspaper *Kokkai* from 1893 to 1895. Rohan experiments with a complex structure as well as all-encompassing subject matter and a profound theme, observing life less with the romantic eyes of a poet than the contemplative penetration of a thinker. His primary interest is not so much in individual characters as in man's fate and the correlation between a man's personality and fate.

In "The Introduction to *The Minute Storehouse of Life*" (*Fūryū Mijinzō*) (January, 1893), Rohan clarifies the meaning of the title:

I name this work a "storehouse" (*zō*), for the multitudes of nebulous images that constantly visit my mind are stored in the nightlike darkness created by my pen, to exist faintly in a world of half light and half shadow. It is minute (*mijin*) in size, as small as a speck of dust, alluding to the *Hajin Shukkyō* [out of dust issues the sutra, or connecting thread] chapter of the *Kegon Sutra*. Not being omniscient, however, I cannot perceive in one speck great sutras covering [or a thread connecting] all the Three Thousand Worlds. That is why I add the word *fūryū* ["secular" or "poetic"] to distinguish it from the visions of Buddhas and saints and also to forewarn the reader that I observe the speck with unenlightened eyes merely to weave my petty views of flowers and the moon. (VIII, 3)

In an effort to effectively recreate his visions of the cosmic order, he devised a unique structure known as *renkantai* ("chain-link structure"). Addressing his readers at the conclusion of the first unit, he elucidates:

This novel is written not so much for the benefit of the reader as for its own sake. Yet, I am not so pretentious as to proclaim it my intention to continue writing arbitrarily until my creative urge is simply exhausted. In order to sustain the reader's interest and to satisfy my own need as well, I have invented a technique of unifying a number of separate units into a single immense structure. Each unit may have twenty to thirty chapters or merely three or four. . . . I hope the reader will permit me this prerogative. (X, 208)

Rohan's chain-link structure does not consist simply of numerous anecdotes strung together by the presence of pivotal characters, such as Prince Genji in the *Tale of Genji*. In form it is similar to Balzac's *La Comédie Humaine* and Zola's *Rougon Macquart Novels*,[1] in that each unit has its own characters with or without commonly shared personages. Shinoda Hajime, a contemporary scholar of comparative literature, calls our attention to the fundamental difference between the French analogs and *The Minute Storehouse of Life*: each unit of Zola's and Balzac's series can boast its own distinct individual cosmos, sometimes complementing or contradicting one another, and in the process serves to intimate an overriding comprehensive view of life; as a contrast, all the units in *The Minute Storehouse of Life* are actually delineations of a fixed concept unifying and propelling them.[2] In other words, whereas the French approach is inductive, Rohan's is deductive, not only in this novel but in most of his works, except perhaps his very last ones.

Rohan seems to have derived inspiration mainly from Oriental sources. As a literary precedent, Chinese poetry of the T'ang period offers a chain-link structure that consists of Unit A, B, C, . . . A. Rohan's structure, however, is different; instead of a circle starting with A and returning to A, Rohan's Unit A links with B, B in turn with C, and so forth, while all the units are interrelated by some implied connection with two pivotal characters. (This may resemble Japanese *renga*, or linked-verse, but an entire *renga* sequence is unified only vaguely by a mood or a tone, except for a close relationship extending over any three immediate links, which would produce

two complete poems.)³ Aside from the Chinese example, with
which Rohan was doubtless well acquainted, he seems to have
conceived an idea of his own inspired by a Japanese writer.
Earlier in 1890, Rohan observed that Saikaku's stories were
"like a necklace made of jewels each different from another
strung together by a thread—a single theme or purpose" (XV, 7).

For Rohan, the chain-link structure was a literary device
which would enable a writer to provide an insight into the true
nature of life. A well-known quest of knowledge is undertaken
by Zenzai Dōji, a bodhisattva-errant as it were, whose series
of visits to fifty-three wise men and women as he pursued
moral wisdom is recounted in the *Kegon Sutra*. Rohan introduced two episodes out of the fifty-three, in *Isāna's Garden*
(1915) and *Spring Night's Tale* (1916). Zenzai's peregrination
begins and ends with Manjusri, the bodhisattva of wisdom and
intellect, who sets Zenzai on his quest rather than providing
ready answers himself. On the popular level, Buddhist time is
seen as an infinite, eternal flow in which there takes place the
transmigration of souls—endless cycles of birth, death, and rebirth. By means of the chain-link structure, therefore, Rohan
intended to recreate life as a vast framework embracing numberless units of human interrelationships within individual cycles,
and a metaphorical reservoir of knowledge.

In *The Minute Storehouse of Life*, Rohan presents life as it
is, rather than as it ought to be (as he did in his idealistic
phase); and through poignant observation and realistic descriptions, he tries to delineate the karmic law manifested in human
life. The thread through all the units of this novel is the true
meaning of life. Rohan believed in a mysterious, indisputable
law of nature: insofar as man is part of nature, the only salvation for him lies in recognizing and accepting it; and man's
life is meaningless as long as he is ignorant of this law. *The
Minute Storehouse of Life* is a panorama of life in which
characters are helpless victims of their own worldly attachments, typical of which in this case is love.

The first unit, "Bamboo-leaf Boats," introduces a hapless
boy Shinzaburō and a cheerful little girl Sayo in a quiet village
in Kazusa (present-day Chiba Prefecture) around 1874. It
opens with the visit of a monk, Shinzaburō's relative, who used

to be in love with Sayo's now-widowed mother. This unit is memorable for its sympathetic and charming descriptions of children at play. Already the theme of love appears in its evil, harmful aspect as well as in an innocent, redeeming one: Shinzaburō and his ailing grandmother are about to be dislodged from their home by the mercenary stepmother, whose amorous hold changed his hard-working kindly father into a greedy, slothful man; but gentle, loving Sayo can dispel Shinzaburō's contrary and gloomy mood.

The second unit, "Thin Ice," and the third, "Dayflowers," concern Sayo's young uncle who boards a ship at Yokohama for China determined to make a name for himself, leaving behind a young woman who pleads pathetically to accompany him. The long speech of Sayo's mother, admonishing her nephew against his reckless lust for adventure and his espousal of heroism, seems to reflect Rohan's critical attitude toward the youth of the day who were feverishly rushing to reach the Continent in the face of an imminent war between China and Japan. "Horseshoes," Unit 4, describes a scene in which a comrade of Sayo's uncle intercedes in an argument between a proud blacksmith in Yokohama and two American customers over the shape of horseshoes. This comrade is a Rohanesque tall, masculine man who speaks fluent English, a rather typical Meiji political activist; but neither a political nor a love theme appears in this light, comic unit.

The fifth unit, "The Lotus-leaf Cup" (a cup used for farewell drinks), returns to the friendship between Sayo and Shinzaburō, who is about to become an apprentice in Tokyo, with most poetic and moving scenes of children fighting and playing together. After his grandmother's death, a constantly leering unsociable Shinzaburō and a concerned Sayo come upon a small dragonfly struggling in a net woven by a multicolored spider. While Sayo frantically tries to release the dragonfly, Shinzaburō dashes it to the ground and strikes a girl who has killed the spider. As the death of the fragile insect forebodes, cruel vicissitudes of life await Shinzaburō after he parts with Sayo.

Unit 6, "Beach Pines of Kiku," is set in Kokura, Kyushu, where Shinzaburō's relative (the monk) returns from his visit to Kazusa.

The life of a young acolyte at the temple is described humorously. Cast against the cheerful hopeful mood at the temple is a fatalistic account of an unfortunate love triangle in the household of a brush vendor dealing with the temple: the brush vendor, his wife, and her lover are caught in psychological, emotional, and circumstantial webs not necessarily of their own making until the wife is divorced, her ex-lover leaves town, and the husband turns into a profligate. At the end, the young acolyte paints on a wall what he defines as a picture depicting the truth, "All who meet must part," which is one of the central tenets in *The Minute Storehouse of Life*.

Unit 7, "The Small-wheeled Cart," tells the story of Shinzaburō's employer (Kizō), a homely but diligent self-made man who inherited his master's grain store. The master's beautiful daughter (Kono) had married a handsome but inept man against her father's deathbed instruction to wed Kizō. The eighth unit, "A Useless Sickle," relates her love affair, her scheming, and her sorrowful life after the death of her husband. Her daughter is about to be sold into prostitution by an evil employer but is saved by a righteous robber. Out of youthful admiration, the girl's young brother accompanies the robber on his way to burglarize the grain store where Shinzaburō works. The boy alone is apprehended because Shinzaburō finds a fallen letter which identifies the boy. In these two related units, characters are at the mercy of the karmic law, acording to which each reaps his own due of good or ill. Shinzaburō as an unrelated party is instrumental in bringing about the reencounter between his once wronged master and the reduced woman pleading for the release of her son. Kizō gives an impression of being an unjustly maltreated, innocent and capable man in the Unit 7, but after he becomes a success in the Unit 8, he appears somehow crude and petty. Kono, on the other hand, changes from a spoiled rich girl into a brave, chaste, and attractive widow and mother in her poverty. Such examples abound in Rohan's works, reflecting his basic belief that greed and material comfort reduce a man to ignoble trivialism.

The ninth unit, "Seagulls," finds Shinzaburō living in the house of Sayo's relative as a household helper. The story focuses on the son of the family who falls in love with a courtesan, the daughter of a bankrupt shipping merchant. The emotion-filled letters they exchange are stylistically superb and comprise almost one half of this unit. Their love is destined to remain unconsummated under the circumstances, and the story ends with the courtesan's letter expressing her hope that they will have a completely fresh start in their next life.

Unfortunately, this is the end of *The Minute Storehouse of Life* as we have it today, for this novel was never finished. In 1894, typhoid fever almost claimed Rohan's life. During his convalescence, the Sino-Japanese War broke out, and his mind was occupied with concern for the safety of his brother. (Lieutenant Gunji was struggling in the Kurile Islands to survive against overwhelming odds—scarce provisions, shortage of vessels, incomplete housing, and the severe climate.) At this point, moreover, Rohan was again assailed by ever-growing doubts about the intrinsic value of fiction. A man of sincerity who demanded no less personal integrity of himself than of his characters, Rohan refused to compromise with his own standards. Painfully he apologized in a preface to the eighth unit:

An author must be inspired enough to deliberate over his ideas and refine his style. Otherwise, not only will his endeavor be reduced to a sordid enterprise purely for monetary gain or fame, but his novel itself will turn into a detestable fraud. I may have written poor works in the past, but luckily I was never forced to create a fraud. Now for the first time I am about to taste the bitterness of such a misfortune.

To confess the truth, not only do I feel uninspired but I have begun to find less enthusiasm for fiction. . . . No matter how hard I try, nothing but a deep sigh rises from within me. I beg my reader's forgiveness for my decision to cast aside the pen and exit from the world of poetry. At this time when even farm boys and old fisherwomen turn their hearts so unselfishly to the fate of our nation, how shameful of me to go on with such idle regrets. . . . My body may have recovered, but is my soul still ailing? (X, 212–13)

This novel covers only the childhood of the two pivotal characters (Shinzaburō and Sayo), less than one quarter of the vast scheme originally intended. The major portion of the planned novel was supposed to deal with the adult life of Shinzaburō and Sayo with all other characters reappearing, involved in the lives of the two.[4] In its existing form in 447 pages, nevertheless, this story presents no less than 133 characters, including more than thirty-five major ones.[5] Especially remarkable is the fact that many memorable children appear in significant roles with distinct personalities.[6]

Rohan's first attempt at the chain-link structure thus ended incomplete; and this unique concept had almost half a century to wait before it was utilized again in his last story, "Records of Linked Rings" (1940). Rohan's original intention was to recreate a literary Indra's net—a celestial net of precious jewels described in the *Kegon Sutra* to illustrate the principle of interdependence and interpenetration of all existences.[7] As each jewel reflects the entire cosmos (all the jewels including itself mirrored in all other jewels), each individual's life is interwoven with and dependent upon other individuals.

The Kegon doctrine of reciprocal origination and simultaneity of all existences is explained in the famed Parable of the Golden Lion by Fa Tsang (643–712), the most honored master of the Kegon Sect in China. As the existence of a golden lion depends on the concept of lion and material gold, all things are fundamentally and eternally interrelated and interdependent, nothing being defined without all other things.[8] At this point, the Buddhist cycle is no longer a merely progressive series of repetitions in the time sequence of past, present, and future lives: it symbolizes an organic cosmos in which multitudes of cycles exist simultaneously and intricately interwoven. Thus, there can be no dichotomy between the ideal and the phenomenal. Each phenomenon embraces the ideal in it and vice versa; and each phenomenon symbolizes all other phenomena. Unlike the morality play, in which each character personifies an abstraction, Rohan's characters stand for every man as well as every ideal. From the Kegon point of view, within each man live all the six beings (gods, human beings, fighting spirits, beasts, hungry demons, and the tortured in hell), just as the Three-thousand Worlds of Six Beings cast their images on each celestial jewel in the Indra's net.

Rohan elucidates man's existence in the universe by means

of poetic imagery. In the preface to an essay collection, "Floating Dust" (1889), he remarks that a shaft of light leaking through a small chink resembles a roll of white silk hung from the sky. Basically incorporeal and transparent, light is turned into a visual phenomenon by innumerable specks of dust deflecting it. "Nothing exists independently.... Sunlight and floating dust join to assume the white color. All poetry is but materialization of floating dust" (XXXII, 62). The imagery of dust, of course, is frequently found in various sutras. The *Kegon Sutra* teaches: within each speck of dust lie all the dharma worlds;[9] eternity is reflected in a speck, and a speck in eternity;[10] and one speck contains the spheres of the six beings, all living out their respective karma.[11] For Rohan, therefore, man is a speck helplessly floating among, and dependent on, all other existences.

As the *Kegon Sutra* compares the human mind to a skillful painter and the universe to his creation,[12] Rohan sees the fate of a man as being determined by his mind. Some modern scholars have even gone so far as to venture a suggestion that the cause-and-effect view of man's fate is actually Rohan's unique interpretation of the subconscious.[13] To a certain degree, it is true. In Buddhist (especially Kegon) idealism, human existence is not merely spatial but also temporal. A man's present existence is charged with his past lives and encompasses his future life; and his subjective cognizance of his existence is at the same time its objective cognizance. (He cannot behold his own existence, a jewel in Indra's net, without simultaneously perceiving all other existences—jewels—which cast their reflection on it.) The absence of conflict between subjective and objective realities, moreover, serves to affirm the truth to be both subjectively and objectively true.

When completed, *The Minute Storehouse of Life* was to reveal the principle of totality (one of the central Kegon beliefs)—that the world can be understood only in its cosmic entirety embracing past, present, and future, as well as all sentient beings. While the Japanese literary world was about to be inundated by the trivia of dark, inconsequential, sordid slices of life in mistaken imitation of Western naturalism, the chain-link structure was one means through which Rohan attempted to maintain his idealistic and lofty visions.

II *The Paradox*

In Rohan's comic play, *The Wealthy Poet* (1894), a minor poet identified as Little Rohan laments that a weak-willed, talentless man like himself is dominated by the taste and fashions of his time and, instead of transmitting "the human gospel," he is reduced to describing the "screams of Hell." Aside from this poignant forewarning to his contemporaries, Rohan's desire to propagate the "human gospel" was perhaps one of the reasons why he wrote stories for youth. Japanese literary historians usually credit Iwaya Sazanami's "Golden Boy" (*Koganemaru*, featuring a fox by that name, 1891) with having heralded the new *shōnen bungaku* ("literature for youth"). A year earlier, Rohan had already written "Tempering of Iron" (1890), in which he compares a boy to crude iron, to be tempered by hardship into a marvelous sword. An impoverished young boy tries to beg for money on the street in order to support his sick father. When a school mate ridicules him for such an ignominious behavior, the boy realizes that he was wrong in expecting something for nothing. So he walks proudly offering his services to anyone willing to employ him. A scholar gives him some money and a book entitled *Jijoron* (*Self-help*),[14] instructing him that a boy's primary work at his present age is nothing other than serious study. Rohan wrote varieties of other works for boys (fiction, biographies of great men, scientific discourses) in his attempt to propagate knowledge, which he deemed indispensable in the development of the mind, and also to provide actual models illustrating the correct way to live.

In *The Wealthy Poet*, Rohan further contemplates on the perplexing paradox of absolute values. Little Rohan is at a loss to learn that compassionate, just, well-intentioned acts can lead to misery and harm. His host, a wealthy and compassionate poet called Jinsai (Master Humanity), lends money to anyone in need. To his dismay, Jinsai discovers what his money has done to the borrowers: one man failed in a business venture and fell ill from worrying constantly over how to repay the loan; another gambled away the money to be put in prison; a poor miller lost sleep for fear of burglars and decided to return the loan.

To compound his distress, Jinsai has a dream in which the horses and cows in his stable are confessing that they are reincarnations of men who once borrowed money from Jinsai and died before repaying the debts. They lament bitterly that had Jinsai adamantly demanded repayment, they would not be forced to repay in service now in such wretched forms. Upon awakening, Jinsai immediately burns all the loan receipts, but the borrowers refuse to accept cancellation of their debts for fear of deeper moral indebtedness. At the end of the play, Jinsai laments as Little Rohan looks on: "What a nuisance money is! I can neither lend it nor give it away without trouble. With this monster called money, I have no idea what to do!" (XII, 60). Since in Buddhist terms, a wealthy man (*chōja*) is at once a man who has accumulated the wealth of virtues, his final realization renders even moral values suspect.

This paradox is probed more extensively in "New Urashima" (1895). Jirō the protagonist is the hundredth descendant of Urashima Tarō, a legendary fisherman who was once granted immortality by the sea goddess for having saved a turtle's life. Tarō enjoyed the sumptuous banquets at the submarine palace of the goddess for a few days and returned at his own insistence to his village. Like the hapless Rip Van Winkle, Tarō found himself a total stranger to everyone except an antediluvian who vaguely recalled the disappearance of a young fisherman during his childhood. According to the traditional version, Tarō in despair opened a mysterious casket which the sea goddess had given him, forbidding him to open it. As the white smoke issued from the box, Tarō turned into a silver-bearded old man of his actual age.

In Rohan's story of a new Urashima, Jirō secretly opens the exquisite box, supposed to have been handed down from Tarō the First. In the morning, Jirō's aged parents are found peacefully lying dead hand in hand. On the way to the funeral service, the corpses vanish leaving behind a jewel in each coffin, one white and the other red. Convinced that his parents have attained the blissful state of immortality by the power of the divine casket, Jirō poses the question whether there actually exist divine beings and immortals. Seven times the yes answer is indicated by the white jewel that he picks up from the box

with his eyes closed. Next he asks if he himself is destined to
attain immortality through the Neo-Taoist *sendō* (the way of
immortality). This time the answer is negative.

Although *sendō* in some ways resemble the heretical black
magic practiced by the medieval alchemists in the West, *sendō*
was also a religion, for its ultimate goal was to produce an
elixir of immortality that could be distributed for universal
salvation.[15] *Sendō* demanded rigorous self-discipline and moral
training as well as alchemical knowledge, and it was considered
a narrow gate through which only a select few could achieve
individual salvation in the form of immortality. At this point,
however, *sendō* is no longer a goal of selfish human desire, but
it corresponds to the unity with the universe that allows men
to transcend time. In such a sense, a desire for immortality
may be similar to the Buddhist wish to return to Amida Buddha,
who is believed to incarnate the Eternal Life (*muryōju*).

Jirō is made to realize that his virtues are not sufficient to
earn him immortality, but then it occurs to him that if there
are gods, there must also be devils. He decides to pay his
respects to a devil, who he thinks must be lonely like an ugly
maiden shunned by all. He performs the Shingon esoteric rite
to invoke the devil. As he recites the magic incantation for the
ninety-eight thousandth time, the earth shakes, thunder booms,
lightning flashes; and a fierce flame bursts forth, most unexpectedly, from his own chest and forms into an enormous
figure of the Demon King. In response to Jirō's request for help,
the Demon King slices Jirō in half to produce an omnipotent
servant called Dōshu (Same Kind), a look-alike of Jirō.

Eventually, however, Jirō is to learn that the attractive
maidens and splendid luxuries that he has been enjoying have
not been magically conjured up but actually abducted or stolen
from nearby towns by Dōshu. Determined to face the consequences of evil deeds that he had unwittingly perpetrated
through Dōshu's services, Jirō orders Dōshu to turn him into
a stone statue. "In his house made invisible by Dōshu's magic
power, the petrified Jirō is said to exist outside of life and death,
faithfully guarded by Dōshu" (II, 273).

The supernatural setting abounding in Rohan's works never
implies an escape or retreat from reality, nor a simple idio-

syncrasy of the author. Such settings (the mountain hut in "Encounter With a Skull," the moon palace in "The Blood-red Star," the palace of the sea goddess and the invisible house in "New Urashima," and the hermitage in "A Sealed Letter") provide a unique sphere in which man confronts his true self and which in the end proves to be the sole reality. Not merely the place but also the time in Rohan's stories is removed from contemporary Japan into the past or indefinite time so that his characters can more plausibly live to the limit of their potential. What appears to be medievalism in his choice of subject matter and setting is his attempt to distill and intensify reality in order to most effectively present the drama of the salvation of man's soul.

Rohan fuses mystic visions and poetic phantasms, unites illusions with truths, and depicts the conflict and harmony between spirit and flesh. In "Encounter With a Skull," reality (which turns a charming maiden into a repulsive leper) and illusion (which materializes a beautiful woman out of a skull) are actually one and the same in the world of truth. It is more profound than the simplistic observation that beauty is only skin deep: in this short work, the identity of the skull shifts from an attractive maiden, an accursed woman, a mad beggar, a revolting leper, and finally to an enlightened spirit. The five-storied pagoda provides a battlefield for the competition between the worldly ambition of Genta and the spiritual aspiration of Jūbei, as well as for the contest between the forces of nature and the power of art (artificial, or human accomplishments). And in "Love Bodhisattva," love (basically a desire of the flesh) and religion (a spiritual yearning) are united in a mystic image of bodhisattva, who is also a Muse. *Fūryūbutsu* (bodhisattva of love and art) as a symbol of the Buddha Nature in man has its antithesis, *fūryūma* ("demon of lust") representing the aspects of man's degradation; and in "New Urashima," Rohan deals with a man's challenge toward the holy and the demonic, both supernatural and leading to the same end.

The concept of the demon in Buddhism has a double meaning. When a man is pitied or denounced for having been bewitched by the devil, the devil or demon refers to human frailty or to the tendency to succumb to the temptation of the flesh. If a man overcomes his weakness, however, he will be able to channel his demonic energy into the pursuit of self-perfection, as do Jūbei, Jirō, Shōzō, and Shu'un. In such a context, the demon is the divine guardian of the Law, fiercely punishing corrupt humans and driving them onto the path of self-purification, just as the *Lotus Sutra* decrees that "the demons shall protect the Law."[16] The King Demon in "The Five-storied Pagoda" and the devouring demon in "A Sealed Letter" are at once an insatiable desire of the flesh, the wrathful punisher of the corrupt and complacent, and the fiery inquisitor of true faith.

The Demon King conjured up by Jirō in an esoteric rite is also a guide to salvation, for by granting Jirō an omnipotent servant who is of Jirō's own flesh, he offers him a chance to face the evil and vanity of human desires. Jirō finally finds freedom in his petrified state, neither spirit nor flesh, for his motive has not been a desperate need to overcome the flesh (emotion) as in the case of other characters but merely an escape from temptations. Outside of life and death in a state of complete inaction, Jirō awaits the time when he can be truly free from his past actions. If "A Sealed Letter" was the record of a twenty-three-year-old Rohan's struggle to resolve the conflict of flesh and spirit, "New Urashima" suggests that at the age of twenty-eight, Rohan had reached a point where the flesh was no longer a formidable threat, rendering it possible for him to achieve spiritual freedom through intellectual self-cultivation. (This work was written two months before his first marriage.)

Yet, human endeavor in attaining freedom is by no means simple; nor is the supernatural world a happy never-never land for Rohan. In contemplating the conflict between this world and the other, between the Buddha sphere and the demon sphere, and between reason and emotion, Rohan examines and questions all moral values. "A Sealed Letter" indicates that the good and evil in human terms by no means correspond to the higher and absolute values: love can be a diabolical obstacle in the process of enlightenment, and a fierce demon can teach the truth by tearing apart illusions.

Furthermore, it is not human values alone that Rohan suspects. The iconoclast in "The Blood-red Star" and Jirō in "New Urashima" distrust even sages and Buddhas. Within the Buddhist traditions, a thorough demythologizing had already been completed by the Zen Sect, which pronounced that sutras were nothing but paper to wipe off filth; that, merely made of scroll, ink, and script, sutras were devoid of any mystic power;[17] and that man must kill Buddhas, arhats [saints in the Hīnayāna], masters, and parents on his way to enlightenment,[18] for such preconceived ideas impede intuitive perception of the truth. Rohan was not only familiar with the Zen teaching but also acquainted with a similar Christian passage. In the preface to his haiku, "How sacrilegious! / Reading sutras with a fan in one hand" (XXXII, 674), Rohan quotes the Bible: "If any man come to me, and hate not his father, and mother, and wife, and children, and brethren, and sisters, yea, and his own life also, he cannot be my disciple" (Luke 14:26). To Rohan, such an attitude meant more than simple detachment from human emotions and obligations, for he saw it as an expression of faith in nondifferentiation, and acceptance, of all things.

It is not forced self-denial that sends Rohan's characters away from reality. It is rather disillusionment and dissatisfaction such as might befall a man upon reaching a certain stage of true knowledge. Kaihi the iconoclast and Genkō the hermit renounce worldly relationships upon realizing the senselessness of their life. Jirō pursues love and success in the beginning, then enjoys fishing in a detached state of mind transcending worldly ambition, next indulges in pleasurable pastimes in a supernatural realm under the sea, but in the end he chooses the immobile quietude beyond life and death. The petrified Jirō has a solemn stateliness reminiscent of the austere and tragic majesty of Dante's Lucifer encased in ice.

It must be remembered that Shu'un ascends to heaven and Kaihi turns into a shooting star. That is to say, all three characters either disappear into space or become part of nature, after overcoming their desires or in order to expiate their sins with profound self-reproach. Their final state is not inactive extinction but suggestive of freedom or potential for perpetual locomotion, for it is charged with infinite kinetic energy. Even Jirō is simply waiting dormant for his existing karma to run its inevitable course so that he can start a fresh life. (The powerful impact of a movement within quietude—a movement which alone defines the world of perception and breathes life into it—had already been captured by Bashō in his haiku: the sound of a frog jumping into an old pond, or a black crow alighting on a withered tree in a desolate autumn scene.)

From a modern point of view, moreover, the real and the supernatural are identical in a curious manner. Jirō achieves a spiritual crystallization by the power of Dōshu, who is his alter ego. When the ego stands for modern materialism and utilitarianism (as does Dōshu), it represents the evil in man propelled by the id, which Rohan called *senshiki* ("submerged consciousness"). In this sense, ego appears to be an antithesis to man's spiritual aspiration. Since Jirō's sublimation is impossible without Dōshu's help, the ego as man's individuality is indispensable in achieving enlightenment. In a peculiar paradox, the subconscious (which strives for the satisfaction of the flesh) is actually the realistic element in man's psyche; and the conscious (*kenshiki*, or manifest consciousness, which aspires toward the world beyond) is the supernatural quality in man, or at least it is in Rohan's view.

For Rohan personally, the supernatural world was not a mere fantasy of the mind but a very real world, if not the only one: the supernatural world, whether or not it actually exists, is a concrete and vivid expression of all-encompassing absolute. Since ideals and romantic poetic visions are inseparably fused in Rohan, the supernatural is true and real to his psyche. The poet Saitō Mokichi observed: "So boundless is my master [Rohan] / Overarching the realm of supernatural / Far beyond this temporal world."[19] Rohan's phantasmal images are, unlike the phantoms in superstitious popular tales, the actualization of visions of the other world. The skull imparts the true bliss in the life after death; the emperor's specter in "This Day" (1898) is an avenging spirit reigning in the sphere of darkness in repudiation of moral compromise; and the apparitions in a sea storm return from the other world to censure Hikoemon the whaler.

In "Supernatural Tales" (1928), Rohan explains the belief in the supernatural, referring to what we would call today "the collective unconscious": "It is not difficult to imagine that the ancient people, more abundant in emotion than in intellect, must have believed and transmitted legends and myths as facts.... Even today, we, the descendants probably still retain a touch of our ancestors' beliefs" (XVIII, 88–89). The preface to "Snowflakes Dancing" attests to Rohan's poetic imagination. In 1889, Rohan was forced to terminate this ambitious epic novel based on Ainu history. Almost a decade later, Rohan had a dream on a wintery night:

Gazing at the vivid silhouette of Mt. Shakotan, I was deeply moved, even in my dream, thinking to myself, "Long ago a beautiful woman wept herself to death on that peak." Awakening, I realized that the woman's death at Mt. Shakotan was not an actual incident but in fact a scene in the last chapter of a novel that I once planned to write.

Dreams often make no distinction of past and present, no division between the real and the imaginary. Yet, the dream in which I sincerely grieved over the tragic death, confusing my own creation and reality, mysteriously reminded me of my novel completely forgotten until that night. (V, 148–49)

It was soon after this dream that Rohan had one of his disciples finish the novel using his original plan.

CHAPTER 8

The Stagnant Phase (1896–1903)

I The Way of the Samurai

IN 1896, when Mori Ōgai returned from his tour of duty as an army doctor in the Russo-Japanese War, he resumed his critical activities through a new magazine published by his literary group, *Mezamashigusa* (*A Literary Alarm Clock*), which soon established itself as the most influential organ of literary criticism in its day. It carried (in issues 3 through 7) a unique fiction review in the discussion format called *Sannin Jōgo* ("Idle Talks of the Three")[1] with Ōgai, Rohan, and Saitō Ryokuu[2] on the panel. Under witty pseudonyms (Rohan's was Datsutenshi— one who escaped from Heaven), the three commented quite mercilessly and satirically on the works of new writers and literary critics. Among the contributions of this panel to the literary world is the discovery of Higuchi Ichiyō, the first major woman writer to grace Japanese literary history since the eleventh century. Especially Rohan spared no words of praise for her best story, "Growing Up," contributing to her richly deserved fame. Ichiyō is perhaps the only major writer to emulate Rohan's idealistic visions and classical style with any degree of success.

Rohan himself embarked on the task of editing a literary magazine *Shin Shōsetsu* (*New Fiction*)[3] in June, 1896. His primary aim was to discover and introduce new writers, and to free literature from the dictates of publishers. Even though he was disillusioned by fiction himself, Rohan the man of letters still hoped that a younger talent might be able to create a new type of literature effectively synthesizing Rohan's philosophical idealism and the fiction genre. Unfortunately, no new writers of impressive caliber appeared on the scene, and the magazine was forced to carry more and more works by already established

120

writers to increase its faltering circulation. Disenchanted and losing enthusiasm, Rohan let Ishibashi Ningetsu take over the editorship only a year and a half later.

Rohan wrote the "Report on the Times" column in every issue, including comments on foreign novelists such as Zola, Tolstoy, and Goncourt. He also urged his fellow writers to organize an Authors' Association to protect their common interests against the Publishers' Association already in existence, citing the examples in England, America, and Germany. (The Japanese copyright law was put into effect in 1899, but Rohan's advice went unheeded until 1946, when the Nihon Chosakuka Kumiai, or Japanese Authors' Union, was formed for the express purpose of protecting authors' rights and interests.) This is one of many occasions on which Rohan displayed considerable foresight in practical matters, far from being an absentminded scholar lacking in worldly wisdom.

In terms of the output and quality of his works of fiction, however, the third period is Rohan's stagnant phase, during which he experimented with the *genbun itchi* style and a realistic approach in a number of short works. Although he did eventually demonstrate a command of the *genbun itchi* style in his later historical biographies, his attempts at realism in this period were mostly unsuccessful. There are, however, three memorable stories, all set in the past and written in *gazoku setchū* (a combination of poetic and vernacular styles): "The Bearded Man" (1896), "Kyūbei the Potter" (1899), and "Tales of Two Days" (1898 and 1901).

The revised and completed version of the 1890 story, "The Bearded Man" is significantly framed in a historical background, as are the other two major works in this period. Probably the objective and exacting nature of history assured Rohan of at least a minimum possibility for writing fiction with a certain intellectual gratification, when he was mentally revolting against the unsubstantial nature of fiction. The setting is the Battle of Nagashino, which took place in 1575 between Takeda Katsuyori (1546–1582) and the combined army of Oda Nobunaga and Tokugawa Ieyasu. Nobunaga (1534–1582) was already an acknowledged power commanding the eastern and central provinces; and after finally destroying Katsuyori in 1582, he would

have become the first unifier of all Japan but for his untimely
death at the hand of a rebellious general. Ieyasu (1542–1616),
moreover, was to establish the Tokugawa Shogunate, which
kept Japan unified under its tight feudal rule until 1867. The
outcome of the Battle of Nagashino, therefore, is as familiar
to Japanese readers as is that of the Revolutionary War to
Americans.

Set in this bloody, strife-torn age of heroes known as the
Period of Warring States, this story presents a fictional warrior
Kasai Dairoku belonging to the Takeda forces. The tragic
implications of his affiliation are doubly intensified by another
historical fact, that Katsuyori's father, Shingen (1521–1573), had
been a formidable and dreaded strategist, on the verge of con-
quering Ieyasu's domain when he succumbed to fatal illness.
The Takeda army under Shingen had come through numberless
battles virtually invincible—a feat in itself not to be claimed
by any other clan. In their encampment at Nagashino, at last,
the high-ranking Takeda retainers were forced to abandon their
shattered dream of ultimate conquest—once almost within their
grasp—to face the cold reality: theirs was an army suffering from
low morale under the wanton leadership of an inept young lord.

Within this historical context, the real issue in "The Bearded
Man" is the question of death. There are three types of death
treated in this story. One reflects the traditional (or generally
believed to be orthodox) view of death that drives the losing
Takeda's elders to the unanimous decision to die in battle as
the last gesture of remonstration toward their weak-willed,
erring lord. The second is the death wish of a young boy in
the Tokugawa army, Kotarō, who forces Dairoku to kill him
in combat for fear that his feeble health might soon prevent him
from performing any act of samurai loyalty to his lord. The
third and the most significant is Dairoku's confirmation of life
strengthened by his acceptance of death.

There are a number of dramatic scenes, including one in which
Kotarō's lovely sister attacks Dairoku to avenge her brother's
death. In a sitting position and with a sheathed sword, Dairoku
intercepts her desperate blows but soon subdues her under
the knee after allowing her blade to strike into his shoulder.
This sister is also a Rohanesque heroine with a fiery spirit and

an unswerving sense of justice shrouded in perfect femininity, a female version of an ideal samurai. The solemn and irrevocable fact of Kotarō's death, nevertheless, allows for no hint of romance with the tall, muscular, black-bearded hero who exacts begrudging admiration even from his enemy, Nobunaga.

To the humanist Rohan, not only man's soul but man's biological life in itself was sacrosanct and precious. His characters rarely commit suicide, especially for the sole purpose of escaping from agony or to ease their conscience. When the warrior Dairoku overhears the high-ranking vassals discussing the impending battle, he cries out literally in tears:

Why are you all so anxious to go to your death tomorrow? How deplorable! Granted our lord seems to grow more irrational by the day, taking advice only from dishonorable flatterers against appeals of loyal officials. You must have decided to die rather than live to see our lord's house ruined by the devil-bewitched young man. You may just as well choose life, don't you see? I believe this to be the very moment when a man and warrior must fight to live. Won't you change your mind to fight for life rather than for death? (V, 316–17)

On the following day, the Takeda army loses the battle as predicted. An elder, who is Dairoku's uncle, exchanges the last words with Dairoku in the battlefield:

I sent off the lord on my horse which had a little more life left in him. . . . I assume you have some worthy causes for which to prolong your presence in this world, seeing how sincerely you tried to convince us to do the same. Have no fear, my nephew, for your old uncle won't fail in death, and I trust you won't fail in life, either. (V, 356)

The aged uncle goes off to join the rear guards, and Dairoku leaves the battleground vowing to live his life to the full. He is later captured in an attempt to kill Nobunaga, but eventually escapes to join the Takeda army in their last and fateful battle of 1582.

This is a surprising departure from the common interpretation of the code of warriors that taught, "The way of the warrior lies in dying."[4] But a careful study of *Hagakure* (the Nabeshima Clan house codes recorded around 1716) reveals that Rohan's interpretation is accurate. In the context of this "samurai bible" deemed to be an expression of the orthodox *bushidō* (the way of the samurai), the meaning of "dying" is threefold: for one, it signifies a speedy spontaneous act from pure motive not contingent upon the consideration of possible consequences; second, it is to enrich and enlarge the possibilities of one's existence to their maximum by dying a figurative death every morning and evening and to take responsibilities at the risk of one's life; the third is selfless devotion and service to one's lord.[5] The last meaning may at first glance seem feudal in nature, but it is inexorably related to the concept of *jihi* (Buddhist compassion), for *Hagakure* lists as one of the warrior's four sacred pledges, "A warrior must practice Great Compassion to serve people." Dying, therefore, meant that a warrior must be ever ready to serve others even at the cost of his own life. *Hagakure* itself explains: "Dying simply means that when the choice is life or death, the samurai should choose death without hesitation, precisely because man's natural inclination is toward life."[6]

Rohan's firm stand against an impulsive urge to die corroborates his disapproval of the suicide fad (condemned as "Wertherism" by *Waseda Bungaku* in 1892) sweeping across Japanese intellectual circles in the wake of the explosive popularity of Goethe's *Die Leiden des jungen Werther* (*The Sorrows of Young Werther*, 1774).[7] Once again in the summer of 1942, when Japan was on the verge of national suicide, Rohan revealed his personal feelings against war in a haiku: "Wrestle about, / You Fighting Spirits, / Over beyond the peaks of cloud" (XXXII, 702). In Buddhist cosmology, a state of battle is punishment reserved for fighting spirits (Asura) and not for man. While Japan turned itself into the sphere of Asura, Rohan wished that fighting would take place only where it belonged— outside of the human sphere.

Some type of death is, nonetheless, vindicable and even obligatory. Rohan's samurai hero may choose life for a cause (Dairoku) but also death for the loss of his mission (Kiken the Rare Man). Rohan wrote a tribute, "General Nogi," in 1912 on the ritual suicide of General Nogi Maresuke (1849–1912), whom Mori Ōgai glorified in his own historical story "The Suicide Note of Okitsu Yagoemon" (1912) as a paragon of *bushidō* ideals for following the Emperor Meiji in death. Rohan saw Nogi's death as comparable to the Crucifixion in its moral implication, but in a Buddhist context. From *Juryōbon* (Infinite Life chapter) of the *Lotus Sutra*, he quotes the Buddha's declaration: "By absenting myself from the world, I caused people to thirst for me. After my death, they worshipped my remains and their hearts craved for me. Thereupon I have come forth to preach the Law."[8]

Rohan advises the reader to comprehend *Juryōbon* through the general's death and his death by the sutra, for "without preaching, the general showed the Way; and without listening, the people heard the teaching" (XXV, 260). By committing *junshi* (the ritual disembowelment of a vassal upon his lord's death), Rohan believed, Nogi reminded the complacent, materialistic modern society of the forgotten virtues such as loyalty. Rohan reserved great respect for a meaningful death, for life itself would be worthless without a purpose and a man without a mission would be worse than a vegetable. Rohan observed, "There are lives, and there are deaths. Some men are living dead, while some dead are alive," and "he who accomplishes his mission lives forever, for such a man is a god. General Nogi is unquestionably a god" (XXV, 260).

Yakuō Honjibon (the origin of the Bodhisattva Yakuō chapter) of the *Lotus Sutra* relates the story of Yakuō, who was formerly called Issai Shujō Kiken Bosatsu (Grateful-Sight-of-All-Beings Bodhisattva) for setting his body on fire to provide the world with illumination (or enlightenment).[9] This episode implies not approval of suicide but rather praise for selfless dedication to the Law. Numerous acts of self-sacrifice are retold in *Jataka* tales (the legends of the Buddha's former lives). One of the most famous is the story of a prince (Buddha in his earlier incarnation) who cast himself down a cliff to feed his body to a hungry mother tiger nursing her cubs.[10] In this light one should remember Jūbei's determination to plunge headlong from the top of the pagoda. Unintentionally though it may be, Jūbei performs the last and utmost religious service, that is, to offer his life to protect the pagoda that is symbolically the Buddha's body itself.

II *The Disillusionment*

Death, on the other hand, may be the only alternative to end a life that has lost its *raison d'être* after a man fails in his mission of mercy. In "Demon of Love," an engraver of precious metal called Heishichi falls in love with Hama, the daughter of his dealer. She secretly makes facsimiles of masterpieces for him, and Heishichi becomes an expert in his art, encouraged by Hama's love and inspired by the superior models. One day an heir to the Gotō family, the most influential in the trade, comes to claim Hama for his mistress. She pleads with Heishichi to elope, but he procrastinates, in consideration of his obligations toward his dependent mother and sister, until Hama is dragged away from his room. After that, he is unable to produce a single piece of work; he is in such anguish because of his broken love and so overwhelmed by the masterpieces (mostly products of the Gotōs). Day after day he sits glaring at them until his fatigued eyes contract a disease and he loses his sight completely. Hama eventually flees from Gotō to Heishichi and, blaming herself for having ruined the brilliant career of a talented artisan, pledges love in their next life. They commit double suicide.

Heishichi regains Hama but his artistic ambition is thwarted forever, for he is overcome by his emotions and overawed by past accomplishments of the human race, unlike the other, successful heroes who sublimate their love (Shu'un), surmount a sense of inadequacy (Shōzō), or transcend social obligations (Jūbei), to challenge the past masters in their own ways. For Rohan, man's life is precious because man is charged with a mission; without a cause, man has no reason to be alive. Kiken the Rare Man is admired for committing ritual suicide after his mission to enlighten the morally complacent samurai class was carried out by the loyal retainers of Lord Asano in spite of Kiken's failure; and having lost his sight and ability to consummate his mission as an artist, Heishichi terminates his own life.

"Kyūbei the Potter" marked the end of Rohan's artisan stories. Its main characters are a potter and a courtesan whose love affair and involvement in "trade espionage" occurred actually in the 1650s. A Kyoto potter Kyūbei begins to seek the favors of a courtesan Matsuyama, after he learns that her father is a debt collector from the Kyushu potters' guild, whose secret of gold-painted porcelain is jealously guarded. Through the help of Matsuyama, he finally induces her unsuspecting father to confide the secret. Kyūbei succeeds in producing a new porcelain even superior to the Kyushu products, but loses his mind after Matsuyama's father is executed for revealing the trade secret inadvertently. He recovers later, eventually to settle down to a happy married life with Matsuyama.

This story offers a highly polished style and intricate psychological study, especially in Kyūbei's maneuvers to influence Matsuyama and her father. A shift toward realism is evident in that Kyūbei is no longer conceived as an exemplary artisan who is a high priest of sacred art but rather as an ordinary man driven by an overriding desire to excel in his trade. (Porcelain products are after all mere utensils, not comparable to a sword regarded as the spirit of the samurai or a pagoda enshrining religious objects.) As fiction became suspect, art and artists might have lost their redeeming symbolism in Rohan's eyes at the same time; and he abandoned the artisan genre thereafter.

The first part of "Tales of Two Days" is entitled "This Day" and deals with the encounter of Saigyō the poet-monk (1118?–1190?) and the vengeful spirit of the retired Emperor Sutoku (reigned 1123–1140), who died in exile following the abortive Hōgen Uprising of 1156 sponsored by his supporters against the power clique behind the reigning emperor Goshirakawa. While Saigyō is reciting the *Lotus Sutra* before the imperial tomb at Shiramine in Sanuki (present-day Kagawa Prefecture), he is visited by the ghost of Emperor Sutoku, former patron of Saigyō the warrior-poet. Saigyō entreats the ghost to free itself from wrath and hatred by accepting the truth that one's enemy is actually one's teacher in achieving enlightenment, just as poisons can be efficacious medicine if administered properly and demon gods are nothing but manifestations of the Buddha. The emperor laughs at Saigyō's ignorance of the fact that Buddha is not to be loved nor are the devils to be despised, for peace is not worth desiring nor is suffering intolerable enough to be shunned. Vowing to destroy all worldly laws and all living souls, the ghost vanishes into a crimson glow.

Saigyō's Shiramine visit is mentioned in a historical war tale, *The Rise and Fall of the Genji and the Heike* (ca. 1250); and *Senjūshū*, a collection of Buddhist lore, erroneously attributed to Saigyō. No ghost appears in these original references, but the romantic nature of this anecdote contributed to its early fictionalization by Ueda Akinari (1734–1819) in *Tales of the Rainy Moon* (1776) and by Takizawa Bakin in *A Curious Tale of the Bow-shaped Moon* (1806–1810), a fanciful *Odyssey*-like adventure romance.

In Akinari's version, the emperor's ghost is appeased by Saigyō's poems and disappears peacefully at dawn. And Bakin alters the story so that the spirit visits Minamoto Tametomo (a tragic hero and expert archer of the pro-Sutoku forces in the Hōgen Uprising) and instructs him to carry out his heroic mission in Kyushu. Rohan, on the other hand, focuses on Buddhist philosophy: if Saigyō is representing the acceptance of all things to achieve release from attachments, the emperor's spirit urges the destruction of all illusions that are the world.

"A mysterious figure, tall and frightfully gaunt" proudly proclaims:

Even the Buddha, who preaches the Law of Salvation, is my enemy now. I refuse to accept Nirvana and release from emotion. Once my enemies robbed me of my life and cast me down into the abyss. Now I shall drown them in tears and bury them in the echoes of my derisive laughter. Who, do you suppose, is causing the chaos in the world? . . . I am the Lord of the Underworld who moves, acts, laughs, and rests in darkness. So long as there is the water of the True Law, how can the waves of Evil cease to surge? . . . Until the time comes when the flashing of crossing swords fill the entire nation and my enemies learn the extent of my anguish as their own, I shall persist in wreaking my vengeance on the court and kindling dissension in the land. (V, 554–55)

Saigyō pleads with the spirit to relinquish his hatred and deliver himself.

"Equality is my foe; discrimination my principle," declared the spirit. "The Buddha is Wisdom; I, Emotion. . . . The world is at my mercy, soon to be turned into the Sphere of *Asura*, my own domain. How gratifying!" His laughter reverberated in Saigyō's ears; and his blazing flames reflected against the mountains emblazoning the universe crimson. (V, 561)

Such is the intensity of the ex-emperor's hatred of evil that he refuses to compromise. If the Sphere of Gods is lower than the Buddha Land in the Buddhist chain of beings, it is still one step above the Human Sphere, where man lives in expedient and complacent compromise with evil. Saigyō's plea goes unheeded because the ex-emperor has already risen above the point of saving himself, and is now able to "discriminate" evil and hate it with passion. Mere forgiveness or resignation comprehensible to Saigyō is not derived from the ultimate knowledge of the true nature of the world and, therefore, is utterly meaningless to the ghost. Though the emperor's view may parallel Rohan's own repudiation of fiction as a means to achieve enlightenment, it is by no means the cynical nihilism of a failure, as made clear by the heroic majesty of the emperor in Rohan's version, in contrast to the submissive or tame spirit portrayed by Akinari and Bakin.

"This Day" is particularly remarkable for its magnificent style heavily studded with Buddhist terms and imagery. As the poet Saitō Mokichi noted,[11] Rohan skillfully fuses the dynamic, staccato, and rhythmic style of the Buddhist sutras with the smooth-flowing, undulatory, unpunctuated, run-on sentences of the Heian novels.[12] In section one, for instance, Saigyō's entire past is narrated in one single sentence extending over three pages. Surprisingly enough, it is not in the least monotonous, owing to the generous use of Buddhist and literary allusions and Chinese compound words. Such a complex style is suitable in a story dealing with characters who actually lived at the beginning of the medieval period, when the feminine Heian literary tradition was in the process of transformation under the influence of the masculine tone of a new warrior-oriented culture.

In this part one of twin stories with a dualistic title "Tales of Two Days," furthermore, dualism does not end with the eclectic style: it is in fact the focal motif of this tale dealing with a number of implied conflicts such as this world versus the other world, the Human Sphere versus the Demon Sphere, and reason versus emotion, each personified by Saigyō and the emperor. In addition, within Saigyō's mind there takes place a clash between mere human awakening and true enlightenment, which may very well mirror the inner conflict of the author himself.

The second part, "That Day," is a tranquil terrestrial antithesis to the violent emotion of the supernatural realm. Saigyō is reunited with his long-deserted wife at the Hase Kannon Temple. He tells her not to be shackled by her love of their daughter, for "it is human nature for parents to anguish over their children, but trying to gratify a child's immediate need is a useless folly" (V, 574). The wife learns that severing delusory human relationships is in fact a true act of love, because it will hasten the child's enlightenment by showing her the true nature of life. If, therefore, Rohan more or less abandoned fiction, it was in search of a better means to achieve the same end.

CHAPTER 9

The Syncretic Phase (1903–1919)

I Waves Dashing Against Heaven

THERE was to be one more major attempt at fiction in Rohan's fourth period, during which he synthesized realism and idealism, *gazoku setchū* and *genbun itchi* styles, poetic qualities and scholarly learning, and more fundamentally, fiction and academic criticism. His experiments in realistic techniques culminated in *Waves Dashing Against Heaven* (1903–1905), which was welcomed by the literary world with immense enthusiasm. Yet this novel was also fated to remain unfinished. As if to prove Rohan's own theory of the cyclic nature of life, first influenza interrupted the serial; and as he recovered, another war broke out in 1904, this time the Russo-Japanese War. Again he wrote a public letter to his readers, demonstrating his literary conscience:

I firmly believe that whether in war or in peace, being loyal to one's own trade means at once being loyal directly to one's own country. . . . To reveal the plot as I planned it, this novel is about to enter into a chapter involving a woman and consequently infused with the scent of rouge and powder. . . . I cannot find it in my heart to write amorous scenes for a public newspaper at this time, when a soldier is going off to war the day after his wedding, or another is leaving an old mother and young children in care of relatives. . . . In short, I believe that my freedom of creative choice cannot be compromised in the least by the conditions of the world, but I am also convinced that inasmuch as my work is meant for public consumption, it is only proper for me to take social situations into consideration. . . . (X, 221–22)

When the war was nearing its victorious end, Rohan tried to resume the serial but again postponed it due to his anxiety

131

over the capture and imprisonment of his brother in Russia. Later the novel was continued intermittently until finally abandoned unfinished in 1905.

Waves Dashing Against Heaven concerns seven young men who make a pact to achieve success each in his own way. They all come to Tokyo and realize their dreams—becoming a ship's captain, a stock speculator, an army lieutenant, a journalist, etc. The finished portion in 462 pages deals chiefly with one of them, Mizuno, who alone has not accomplished his ambition, that is, to write but a single poem to offer to the world. He is a school teacher hopelessly in love with a woman colleague who is critically ill but somehow loathes him, refusing even to receive his help. When Mizuno in desperation begins to supplicate gods and bodhisattvas, he is dismissed from his post as a superstitious regressionist unfit to teach. In his financial and emotional crisis, a beautiful and sympathetic woman appears to help him. Just as this woman goes to live with another attractive woman who is the mistress of an influential industrialist, Rohan laid down his pen.

The comradeship of the main characters may seem to echo the Chinese romance *All Men Are Brothers* or Bakin's most ambitious work, *Hakkenden* (*Romance of the Eight Dogs, or the Eight Swordsmen*, 1813–1841). Rohan, nevertheless, acknowledged a much more current inspiration. In 1898, sixteen members of Hōkōgikai (Lieutenant Gunji's associates) were rescued from a deserted South Sea island called Pelham Reef north of Hawaii, where they had barely sustained life for a half year following a shipwreck.[1] Rohan, who knew them personally, read their captain's log with great interest.

In his 1900 article, "The Ocean and Japanese Literature," Rohan laments the absence of true "sea literature" in Japan—an archipelago. In Rohan's own words, *Waves Dashing Against Heaven* was intended to be a study of an intellectual, modern-day, Japanese Robinson Crusoe.[2] The central character Mizuno was to commit a murder and leave Japan in a ship commanded by his friend; and they would be forced to live on a desolate island after a shipwreck. Rohan chose seven men of different professions to represent various aspects of the capitalistic, utilitarian Meiji society so that the descriptions of their aggressive and dynamic life would amplify the contrast with the major portion of the story, in which human existence isolated from civilization would be explored with dramatic effects and psychological depth.[3]

Rohan's last novel yielded two new literary devices. One is his style effectively harmonizing a softened classical language in the narrative portion with vernacular employed in the dialogues. The other is a new technique in characterization. Isoko, who is the primary motive for Mizuno's actions, is never once described directly: she is presented only through the references made by other characters or Mizuno, who is in fact constantly barred from seeing her in her sick bed from the beginning of the story. Even though she is decisively a moving force, her personal features and emotions are rather nebulous, except for her intense dislike of Mizuno. It was Rohan's intention to keep Isoko a "shadow character" by means of this unique presentation to the end of the originally planned novel.[4] Mizuno himself, moreover, is a new type of protagonist for Rohan: unlike the massive and sanguine heroes of earlier works, Mizuno's "face is sallow, his slanted eyes murky, and under his thin long nose, his pale straight lips are tightly drawn as if never to open again. Though his features are grimly handsome, he has an air about him that would frighten a child to tears" (IX, 23).

Waves Dashing Against Heaven would have been an ambitious modern version of *The Whaler*, for Mizuno's voyage was to be undertaken so that he would be able to pass a severe judgment on his entire being, to give a definitive interpretation of his existence, and eventually to kill himself in compliance with a self-pronounced death sentence. Mizuno is still an ideal character inasmuch as he reflects the self-analytical conscience of the Meiji intellectual youth, but he is more realistic and human than the Rohanesque samurai and artisan heroes, in his painful self-doubt, emotional anguish, and helplessness.

II *Metempsychosis*

In this unfinished novel, Rohan briefly touches on the Buddhist concept of *rinne tensei* ("metempsychosis") through which man may potentially retain the identity of everyone and knowledge of everything beyond his present immediate experiences. A man with a responsive faculty, therefore, may be able to perceive a vision of a lifetime in a flash, that is, metempirically; or the memories of his former life may momentarily surface into his consciousness. The poet Mizuno muses on his unrequited love while listening to the distant howl of a dog in the night. He recalls a section in "The Vision and the Enigma" chapter of Nietzsche's *Thus Spake Zarathustra*, where the dwarf observes that "Time itself is a circle," and Zarathustra says: "And this slow spider which creepeth in the moonlight, and this moonlight itself, and thou and I in this gateway whispering together, whispering eternal things—must we not all return and run in that other lane gone before us, that long weird lane— must we not eternally return?"[5] As the dog's howl fades into darkness, Mizuno is bathed in cold perspiration, suddenly sensing that in his former life he was also desperately in love with Isoko and she loathed him to the end, just as in their present life. Not only Mizuno, who has read "a book with a chapter called 'Vision and Riddle,'" but even a young girl and her unsophisticated grandfather agree with a shudder that the dog's howl sounded as if asking them, "Am I not the same dog that you used to know in your former lives?" (IX, 165).

Western readers may detect a number of similarities between Rohan and Nietzsche, such as in their belief in the eternal cycle of life, in their courageous acceptance of the fundamental emptiness and relativity of all existences, and in their faith in the hero. Nietzsche was first introduced to Japan by Tobari Shinichirō in his "On Recent German Literature" (1900) and "Nietzsche and Two Poets" (1902). Since there is no evidence that Rohan had a reading knowledge of German, it is safe to assume that he had had no access to Nietzsche before 1900. As far as can be determined, there is no influence of Nietzsche on Rohan's philosophy of life or concept of hero, which had already been firmly established by 1900.[6]

In his most mysterious and abstruse work, "Clay Image, Wooden Image" (1905), Rohan further investigates *déjà vu* phenomenon and metempsychosis. The protagonist is named Genichirō (First Man of Mystery), who sets out on an aimless journey, unable to conform to worldly values. At a small antique store near Kyoto, his attention is drawn to a torn piece of a letter mounted on lady's kimono material. In the dim light of his inn room, he reads the letter which has neither the beginning nor the ending. Just as he is trying to decipher a few lines of faded script on the reverse side, a fire breaks out in the inn. He escapes but the letter is lost forever. While he is walking toward Kyoto in a state of shock, a woman bodily runs into him on the pitch black road and begs for his protection from her pursuers. He grapples with a ruffian only to be choked into unconsciousness.

When he regains his senses, the woman takes him to a tastefully decorated house and entertains him. He asks, "Who is the master of this house?" "I need not tell you, sir, for you know the answer very well," replies a young servant boy, smiling. Somehow the house, the servant, the woman, and everything seem vaguely familiar, as if he were gradually recovering from temporary amnesia caused by high fever. It then comes back to him that the house is his own and the woman is the courtesan from whom he was separated before they were able to marry in their former life. To a still incredulous Genichirō, the woman shows a little birthmark on her left ring finger and promises to meet him again in her next life.

In the morning, he finds himself lying under a tree with a peasant girl looking down at him. Much younger and shabbily dressed, the girl nevertheless is the image of his former love. The girl is deaf and mute. She points to the exact same birthmark on her finger, and he takes her back to Tokyo as his wife. One day they leave their house together, never to be seen again. In the epilogue, Rohan quotes Genichirō's words:

My wife had died of frustrated love in her former life and was reborn deaf and mute due to the pent-up regret and resentment. Until our reencounter, she was in a dim state without the faculty of hearing or speech, her former self not completely dead nor her present self totally alive.... When I happened to find her last letter and then lost it in the fire, my mind in its agitated state somehow received the mysterious message from the past.... In her anguish, she had killed herself, while I had also died young in violent rage.... Without a doubt, three temporal worlds do exist: those without true perception call them figments of the imagination,

but those who have had actual contact know them as unequivocal
reality. (IV, 164–65)

By what faculty, then, can a man perceive past and future?
The answer may be found in Rohan's treatises, specifically where
he discusses the subconscious mind (*senshiki*) in contrast to the
conscious mind (*kenshiki*). "There were men before us; preceding them were men of yet earlier ages; and so on *ad infinitum*,"
says Rohan. "Within the depths of today's language, thought,
and taste, we find the spirit of the ancient people that has
survived through myriads of generations. . . . Within modern man
breathes ancient man; and within the man of old lived the man
of our time" (XXXII, 31). Without resorting to the collective
unconscious of the post-Jung generation, Rohan was already
familiar with an age-old concept which provided an explanation
for such a mysterious potentiality of the mind. It is the Buddhist
concept of *ālaya vijñāna*, a profoundly complex idea, which
can be discussed here only briefly and strictly in relation to
Rohan's metaphysical scheme.

As an explication of human consciousness, *ālaya vijñāna* is
called *araya-shiki* in Japanese—the quintessence of human mind,
into which all *karma* is engraved and from which all mental and
physical activities originate.[7] In this regard, a good deed with
its beneficial effect is no longer merely an objective truth but
also a subjective truth, for the religious and moral law of cause
and effect exists within the depths of human consciousness.
Araya-shiki is heaven's law as well as the demand of the human
heart, as attested by the Buddha's pronouncement, "I have
come forth to preach the Law, for your heart craved after it."[8]
The Kegon doctrine emphasizes *ālaya vijñāna* as *zōshiki* ("storehouse of consciousness"), the Universal Mind, which embraces
all existences and experiences and which engenders individual
consciousness. This collective unconscious surfaces into the conscious either during trained contemplation (Genkō, Saigyō, and
Jirō), at the moment of abrupt insight (Bansei, Kaihi), or in a
dream in the case of laymen such as Young Rohan and Genichirō.

On the metaphysical level, *ālaya vijñāna* is called *ariya-shiki*
in Japanese, referring to absolute reality in the dynamic process
of manifesting itself as the world of phenomena.[9] A Buddhist

scholar Ōchō Enichi interprets the Abundant Treasure Stupa of the *Lotus Sutra* as the surfacing of the invisible into the visible state and at the same time as symbolizing Past (by the underground whence it springs), Present (by the ground where the worshippers stand), and Future (by the space where the Stupa hangs and into which all the visions and worshippers become suspended).[10] Just as Rohan's five-storied pagoda is a manifestation of the collective unconscious shared by Jūbei and Genta as well as a symbol of the all-inclusive eternal truth, reality and the ideal are fused in *ariya-shiki*, which is at once transcendental and immanent. *Ariya-shiki* as reflected in the Kegon doctrine of mutual causation and correlation is what Seri Hiroaki (a contemporary Rohan specialist) calls the cosmic unconscious[11]—a metempiric, superindividual consciousness, without differentiation of the self and others, or of the beginning and the end.[12]

III *Conflict of the Poet*

After interrupting *Waves Dashing Against Heaven,* Rohan composed a long poem in its place for the *Yomiuri* from March to December, 1904. Its title, *Leaving the Hermitage,* derives from the poet-protagonist's departure from his own poetic, subjective microcosm to find inspiration in the universe.

Initially, the poet glorifies the eternal, free, and all-embracing power of the Muse as opposed to the impermanence and emptiness of the physical world and human life. He declares:

Part I, Chapter 15

> While this world is unsubstantial,
> What joy can it hold?
> While my life is delusory,
> What sorrow can I feel?
> Both lied, the world and I,
> Both erred, the world and I.
> Believing this world to be reality,
> Believing this body to be myself,
> In vain I watched the flight of years,
> Helplessly let seasons roll by.
> Learning at last the evanescence of the world,

Bitterly feeling the frivolity of this body,
To this hermitage I retreated.

(XIII, 131–32)

The poet decides that the fanciful vision (poetry) is actually
reality and that he must give up the world and live in poetry.

Part II, Chapter 30

How august is my Muse!
How beauteous is his land
In the luminous glow of his heart!
There bloom perennial flowers,
There shines the eternal moon.
Within the gate of immortality,
Endless is the spring, so genial.
In the garden of immortality
Spouts the fountain, unceasing.
Gracious ladies in multitude
Flock like soft layers of clouds.
And as the glittering stars,
Assemble heroic men in force.

(XIII, 197–98)

The onset of war generates in his heart a conflict between
the terrestrial and the celestial. In the clamor and confusion the
Muse has departed. Within the poet, Form and Shadow lament:

Part III, Chapter 20

Form: Born not of the same substance,
          Of different minds are we, you and I.
Shadow: Yet, in indelible brotherhood
          Our hearts are bound.
Form: You unable to abandon me,
Shadow: And you powerless to desert me.
Form: As I cherish you,
Shadow: So for you I yearn.
Form: Yet, this eve we face an impasse.
Shadow: Yield to you, I cannot.
Form: Nor can you join me.
Shadow: One is on earth,

> The other riding the skies.
> . . . .
> Sharing the same heart, yet estranged
> By dissimilitude in our substance.
> Form: Woe is us, never to be one.
>   (XIII, 274–75)

A young man on his way to take up arms passes outside the poet's window singing in praise of patriotism and action:

Part IV, Chapter 1

> Written in ink are man's poems all;
> In blood alone is my song inscribed.
> Ideograms formed of my life energy
> Soar and dance in the vast sky!
> Sing not, men, of birds and butterflies,
> For even a man adrift is no stranger to patriotism.
> Two and a half thousand years old, our nation,
> This crisis sets my blood ablaze.
> Would to Heaven that I might write a song
> To rumble like an iron drum
> With the roar of my billowing blood!
>   (XIII, 285–86)

Through the discourse with a strange visitor, the poet realizes that nature, war, people, and everything else is poetry. It is in the physical world that poetry exists; it was wrong of him to have sought poetry only in his own heart. He is about to leave the hermitage to sing of the beauty of living nature. He declares:

Part IV, Chapter 19

> A small hermitage!
> What is this small hermitage?
> From this retreat I shall depart
> To lift my sight far yonder.
> Rejoice and sing at a time of peace,
> Mirror the days of war also in song.
> Reality is poetry; so also is fanciful vision.
> A small hermitage!
> What is this small hermitage?

This is not the sole abode of the Muse.
Wheresoever between Heaven and earth
Does the God of Poetry fail to dwell?
At last have I discerned
The whole universe to be the Palace of the Muse.
Standing beside the hermitage, I admire in awe
The universe so alive before my very eyes.
                                                    (XIII, 344–45)

Leaving the Hermitage was Rohan's attempt at creating a national poetry (*kokushi*) to sing the poetic thoughts of the Japanese in the language of the Japanese, at a time when the so-called new style poetry (*shintaishi*) was deliberately imitating Western models. The new style poetry (written in classical poetic diction but not in the traditional short forms such as haiku or *waka*) originates with *Shintaishishō* (1882), a collection of Western poems in translation and some original Japanese poems. The term *shintaishi* was invented by Rohan's friend and philosopher, Inoue Tetsujirō (1855–1944), who stated in the preface to "Song of Life" in this collection that Meiji poetry must be poetry of Meiji Japan, not Chinese poetry nor Japanese classical poetry. Even though *shintaishi* still relied on the traditional Japanese 7–5 or 5–7 meters and poetic styles, its devotees were strongly inclined toward romanticism, as typified by Shimazaki Tōson, who betrays the influence of such English poets as Shelley and Wordsworth. Gotō Chūgai extolled *Leaving the Hermitage* in his article "My First Encounter with National Poetry" (*Shin Shōsetsu*, May, 1904), defining national poetry as poems that have the power to communicate sincere emotions and sincere thoughts through the indigenous, living language.

Leaving the Hermitage is a significant and even a unique poem in terms of the stylistic innovations and philosophical concepts integrated into it. This poem in 267 pages utilizes all manner of poetical devices and styles: Chinese parallel construction, haikulike cryptic expressions, Japanese meters; stanzas and chapters and parts of varied lengths; mixture of diction—classical, literary, vernacular, Chinese, abstruse; varieties of forms—verses, narratives, dialogues, antiphonic songs, lyric poems; characters of all types—gods, goddesses, children, youth, old men, poets, hermits, soldiers, shadows, visions.

Issues are also diverse. The impermanence of the universe is attributed to a mythical lady in Part I, who healed Heaven's battle scars with a medicine made of five stones kneaded together. She thereby gave the universe sincerity (the white stone), compassion (blue), beauty (red), hope (yellow), and strength (black), but she overlooked the permanence of the colorless stone, which never takes on other colors nor loses its own transparency. In Part II, every man is a knot in nature's net called the world, ineluctably related to every other man and affected by others' movements, just as Indra's net in the *Kegon Sutra* illustrates. The moral crisis of the poet at the time of national emergency is dramatized in the dialogue between the Shadow (aspiring toward celestial visions of poetry) and the Form (stirred by its body made of the country's very soil) in Part III. In the final part, the conflict is finally resolved by the realization that poetry is the impermanent world as it is, not because a thing is more beautiful by reason of its impermanence, but simply because the universe is poetry in itself as it is.

This poem may appear to be a confutation of art-for-art's-sake views and an affirmation of naturalistic approaches to literature, but it must be remembered that Rohan had never taken any antinaturalism stands. If the naturalist writers were trying to depict the sordid dark aspects of reality, as they were in Japan, Rohan was seeking to exemplify in his works such ideal characters as actually lived in Meiji society. Since there was no Platonic ideal world apart from reality for Rohan, his idealistic stories were at once products of his objective study of the world, long before naturalism came into vogue in Japan, and *Leaving the Hermitage* must be considered a summation of his consistent belief rather than a declaration of change.

This poem was translated in 1925 by Nagura Jirō and published in London with considerable success. In its introduction, Foster Damon notes, "*Leaving the Hermitage* is but one product of a big movement: the contemporary Japanese search to find the national soul. The profounder ethical issues of life are at present being re-examined and re-defined. How far-reaching, even popular, this search has been is proved not only by the success of this book but by the still greater success of the young Kurata Hyakuzō.... *Leaving the Hermitage* may be considered a psychological novel, the details of which are too subtle for prose. Its problem—the duty of the poet during wartime—is one which recurs again and again in all countries."[13]

As Rohan's biographer, Yanagida Izumi, objectively puts it, however, this poem is not exactly belauded by Japanese literary historians. It is probably due to an overall impression of contrived artistry, monotony, emotional distance arising from too ingeniously devised structure, and sometimes didactic tone, despite certain impassioned sections, such as the young soldier's song quoted above. It is rather ironical that Rohan has been acclaimed more as a poet than a novelist by virtue of intensely poetic qualities in his fiction but not necessarily based on his accomplishments in poetry as such.

In 1908, Kyoto Imperial University appointed Rohan as a lecturer in Japanese literature. His appointment caused excitement in literary circles as an unprecedented tribute to an unquestionably learned yet entirely self-taught man of letters. He lectured four hours a week on *Soga Brothers' Revenge* (fourteenth century), *Wasan* (Japanese Buddhist hymns), the domestic plays of Chikamatsu Monzaemon (1653–1724), and the history of Japanese literature. After the first summer vacation, however, he did not return to the university despite the entreaty of his students, who sent delegates to Tokyo to persuade him. Presumable reasons for his resignation are his distaste for jealousy expressed by others over the highly coveted position he occupied, inconveniences of living alone away from home, and boredom with Edo literature after one year of teaching it. (Rohan's diary entry of May 26, 1916, reveals: "Weary of Edo literature since Kyoto, I declined to join the Edo literature preservation association" [XXXVIII, 360].)

Thereafter, nevertheless, Rohan's standing as a scholar was indisputably established so that the honored doctor of literature degree was awarded to him in 1911. When he was notified of his nomination, he wrote in his diary: "My sole desire at present is but for a boat to take me fishing and a house to study in . . ." (XXXVIII, 30). Until the end of his days, he was to be showered with various honors, but his desire to have but a boat and a house of his own was never to be granted, so little rewarded was he financially.

CHAPTER 10

The Last Comeback (1919–1947)

I *"Destiny"*

FROM 1911 on, Rohan wrote highly regarded scholarly discourses, unique historical tales, and didactic lectures for youth until 1919, when he made his last comeback as a fiction writer with the celebrated "Destiny." It graced the first issue of the intellectual magazine *Kaizō*, which paid a high fee for this historical novel, attesting to Rohan's great prestige even after a long absence from the literary scene. "Destiny" is an account of the power struggle between the Chien-wen Emperor (reigned 1399–1402) and the Yung-lo Emperor (reigned 1403–1424) of China's Ming Dynasty (1368–1644). The characters are all male—emperors, princes, court advisors, generals, and high officials—entangled in a plot to seize the imperial throne. The title refers to the karmic law of nature by which certain causes inevitably generate certain consequences, and the story begins with a question: "Does destiny exist as an actual force?"

First, Rohan mentions Bakin's *Romance of Cavaliers* (1832–1835) recounting the exploits of a royalist beauty who led an army in support of the Southern Court during the dual court period in the fourteenth-century Japan. Then, he introduces Bakin's source, *The Popular Biography of a Lady Mystic* (*Nu-hsien-wai-shih*, 1703–1706) by a Chinese by the name of I Wen-chao, which is a mythical account of the life of T'ang Sai-erh—a Joan of Arc figure who is said to have been called to arms by mystic visions and a precious sword in 1421 against the Yung-lo Emperor. Rohan cautions that the actual uprising of T'ang Sai-erh had nothing to do with the imperial succession struggle and that I Wen-chao turns her into a heroic figure by crediting her with the righteous cause of aiding the Chien-wen

Emperor, who was believed to be alive at the time according to popular sources.

Rohan proceeds to narrate the orthodox account of the imperial power play based on the official history of the Ming Dynasty, *Ming Shih*. The first Ming emperor enfeoffed his many sons with potent armies and extensive authority, naming his grandson as his successor instead of his ambitious favorite son Prince Yen. After the death of the powerful first emperor in 1398, the second emperor Chien-wen's advisors began to find excuses to deprive imperial princes of their royal standing or even to execute them outright. Partly in self-defense, Prince Yen raised an army, took over the throne in 1402, and became the Yung-lo Emperor.

Rohan also discusses Yung-lo's chief advisor Tao-Yen and Chien-wen's counsel Fang Hsiao-ju, speculating on their personality traits on the basis of their poems, discourses, and historical records. As for the monk Tao-yen, who instigated Prince Yen (to whom he owed no particular loyalty) against Chien-wen (toward whom he bore no animosity), Rohan suggests that his un-Buddhist-like conduct was not motivated by a personal ambition; rather, it was simply a natural expression of his latent heroic spirit which surfaced upon chance contact with equally indomitable Prince Yen, as evidenced by many impassioned references to heroes found in Tao-yen's writings. On the other hand, Rohan praises Fang Hsiao-ju as a true *kunshi* (Confucian scholar-gentleman-statesman) who remained unflinchingly faithful to his principles until his brutal execution by the order of Yung-lo.

As for the fate of Chien-wen, Rohan favors an unorthodox but persistently surviving theory that Chien-wen escaped to live out his life as a monk. According to the *Ming Shih*, the empress perished in the palace fire during the final assault by Prince Yen, but Chien-wen's end is unconfirmed. Rohan points out inconsistencies in the *Ming Shih* itself: an entry in its Volume 143 indirectly denies the rumor of Chien-wen's escape; Volume 304 records that Yung-lo sent Cheng Ho (an envoy-explorer) abroad a number of times to demonstrate China's power but, Rohan suspects, probably to search for Chien-wen as well; and also Volume 299 mentions an expedition dispatched under the pretext of finding a mystic in the mountains to obtain the secret of immortality—a most unlikely undertaking for a man of Yung-lo's intelligence and practical mind.

Rohan notes that considering the uneasy balance of power existing at the time in the Yunnan area and the menace of Tamerlane in Central Asia, an escaped Chien-wen and his alliance with foreign powers would have posed a serious threat to Yung-lo. Cheng Ho (who was sent to the present Viet Nam area during the period 1405–1407 and to other Southeast Asian countries during 1408 to 1411) was a eunuch in direct service to the emperor, and the search party for a mystic was headed by a court attendant—both most likely choices, observes Rohan, to be entrusted with secret missions rather than legitimate expeditions.

Even more fascinating is Rohan's account of Chien-wen's escape. At the crucial moment, Chien-wen found in a casket (the first emperor's keepsake) three sets of monk's garb and official identification cards. The first emperor had been a monk before he freed China from the Mongol rulers; by a mysterious turn of the wheel of fortune, Chien-wen saved his own life by means of monastic disguise. A cyclic pattern of fate also visited Yung-lo's son, who was executed for his attempt to usurp the throne from his nephew, the Hsuan-te Emperor, in 1426.

Rohan's view of fate is singular in that he interrelates psychological study of each character with an immeasurable flow of natural forces presumably directed by the karmic agency. Popular sentiments have usually been with the loser and legitimate emperor, Chien-wen, as seen in *The Popular Biography of a Lady Mystic*, but Rohan is objective or even sympathetic toward Yung-lo, who somehow emerges a Rohanesque hero. Supported by historical records, Rohan describes Yung-lo as a man of "masculine features with an imposing beard as well as of great wisdom, courage, and insight; while Chien-wen was graceful, learned, indecisive, and oversensitive" (VI, 207).

Rohan's interest is focused on the interaction of Yung-lo's heroic spirit (which seems to qualify him as a more desirable sovereign than Chien-wen) and karmic law (which by nature must engender a just consequence for any man's action). Rohan questions: "Within four years, Prince Yen fulfilled his ambition. Was it by Heaven's sanction? The will of the people? Fate?

Forces of circumstances? Or, was it not exactly as it should have been?" (VI, 253).

Regardless of whether or not Chien-wen actually survived until he was invited back to the palace in honor by Hsuan-te's son (as popular belief has it), Rohan's position is made clear in the postscript: "If one should accept Yung-lo's success and Chien-wen's death in defeat as Heaven's Will, it would appear as if Yung-lo were guiltless and Chien-wen virtueless. Historical facts such as the peaceful rule within and the prestige abroad of the great empire of Ming China can be accounted for only by the mysterious legend of Chien-wen's eventual restoration and Yung-lo's untimely death" (VI, 314). (Yung-lo died in his war camp under suspicious circumstances.) According to the Confucian belief in government by personal virtue, "a government is good when those near are happy and those far are attracted,"[1] and also "if a ruler himself is upright, all will go well without imposed orders. But if otherwise, his orders will not be obeyed."[2] By this belief, the very peace and prestige enjoyed subsequently by the Ming Dynasty seems to testify that justice had been carried out in the lives of Yung-lo and Chien-wen. Since Chien-wen was indisputably the legitimate heir, by heaven's justice he needs to have survived. What Rohan is claiming is not the historical authenticity but the moral inevitability of Chien-wen's restoration.

This work is acclaimed to be Rohan's best by most of his admirers. Tanizaki Junichirō's remark made in 1950 may sum up their feelings:

Ozaki Kōyō's literary life was probably already exhausted by the time of his premature death. Had he lived longer, he might not have achieved a higher level of professional competence. Rohan, by contrast, suddenly and with so much vigor, reappeared on the literary scene after many years of silence, during which time naturalism mushroomed and withered, and Natsume Sōseki (a scholar-writer like Rohan) emerged and died. "Destiny" marked Rohan's comeback. Even to this day, I cannot forget my excitement upon reading it.[3]

Tanizaki goes on to call it fiction above fiction, an epic as well as a historical biography. Then, he summarizes:

Despite its relative brevity, "Destiny" is a grand work . . . containing a cosmos in itself. Its style is the traditional *wakan konkō bun* [a mixture of Chinese and Japanese dictions] but strangely leaves no impression of being outmoded, thanks to its enormous vitality and dignity. It is beyond a mere historian's ability to depict such world-shaking events with their extreme vicissitudes, bringing innumerable great and minor heroes to life as he does. . . . In this day and age when things resembling pages from a mundane diary pass for fiction, this historical treatise is a novel in its genuine sense.[4]

More recently, the contemporary literary critic Shinoda Hajime said of "Destiny":

The modern novelistic theory that a story develops along with the passage of time does not apply to "Destiny," whose title most aptly describes its contents. The author and the reader are both forced to stand in the same vantage point as the god of fate and accept this chain of drama not as a string of passing events but rather as a single whole factual entity which already exists before them. . . . Rohan's novel is always ruled by a sense of space into which all characters and incidents converge.[5]

After "Destiny," Rohan set about writing commentaries on Bashō's *Six Collections of Linked Verse*, which was to take nearly twenty-five years to complete. As the poet Usui Yoshimi said after Rohan's death, the commentaries may have been the last means that allowed Rohan to continue his literary endeavor mobilizing all his learning, intellectual faculties, and philosophical insight within a framework of fiction, after the concept of fiction as an imaginary cosmos had been destroyed by naturalism, at least in Japan.[6] As a consequence, Rohan tends to create his own poetic world inspired by Bashō's poems rather than merely to elucidate poems themselves. His commentaries are a vast monument reflecting Rohan's entire being as a man of letters. With "Destiny" and the Bashō commentaries, Rohan reconciled a seeming conflict or dichotomy between fiction and reality, for in his eyes history was basically fictional accounts of reality, so that fiction might be as real and revealing as reality itself, or at least more so than history.

"Records of Linked Rings," which was written in 1940, borders on the genre of historical biography and that of fiction. In this short work, Rohan was finally able to complete his chain-link structure, which he had tried once before in *The Minute Storehouse of Life*. Its plot as well as its title are based on a philosophical view of the world that karma (fate) is subtle and complex, resembling a chain of linked jewel rings. The characters are historical Heian period personages such as Kamo no Yasutane (the author of *Japanese Records of Rebirth in the Pure Land*), the poetess Akazome Emon (the alleged authoress of *The Tale of Glory*), and the Abbot Jakushō, who died in China after a thirty-year stay. The story moves from Yasutane (who became the Priest Jakushin) to his disciple the Abbot Jakushō (who achieved religious awakening through a love affair), then to Akazome Emon (the wife of Jakushō's cousin who remonstrates with Jakushō against his affair), and finally to Jakushō's Chinese friends. And the thread stringing together all the characters is their dedication to learning and Buddhism.

Those who love "Destiny" also consider the "Records of Linked Rings" one of Rohan's best works. They include Tanizaki, whose *Captain Shigemoto's Mother* (1950) shows the influence of this story. Jakushō, still a layman, stays for days beside the corpse of his beloved mistress, beholding her still beautiful face. When in excess of passion and grief, he kisses her lips, a repulsive odor issues forth to release him from his amorous attachment. The "Contemplation of the Corpse" scene in Tanizaki's work derives from this episode in the "Records of Linked Rings."

II *The Cycle and Microcosm*

During the early Meiji period, when Christianity, which had recently been reintroduced, was spreading, the existence of God was debated both from the theist and the atheist points of view. Atheists were mostly conservative and nationalistic, opposing Christianity as a foreign faith.[7] One objective presentation of atheism was "Atheism" (1882) by Ueki Emori (1857–1892, a theorist of the people's rights movement). Ueki asserts the nonexistence of God from an empirical standpoint: the unknown cannot be God, for if it can, God is destined to be disproved as sciences advance; God cannot exist, therefore, unless he can be ascertained by five senses.[8]

The Christian evangelist Uemura Masahisa published a series of works in 1884 to prove the existence of God by introducing and synthesizing various theories of Western philosophers: man has an inherent aspiration toward the Ideal (Plato); and therefore, there must of necessity exist what Herbert Spencer called "the unseen existence" to be aspired to; and by the inductive reasoning of John Stuart Mill, the order and the harmony in the universe testify to the presence of an omnipotent God. Uemura also inferred the moral nature of God from the basic goodness in man, referring to Kant, who regarded the human conscience as the proof of God's existence. Uemura also refuted atheism on the grounds of the limitation of man's cognitive faculty: not being omniscient, man can never deny God's existence unless he himself becomes a god.[9]

Sometime before the age of twenty-one, Rohan wrote a philosophical speculation entitled "Mystery of Magic Squares." In its last chapter, "Conclusion," he poses a question whether man's knowledge is finite or infinite:

Those who believe in the existence of God (or gods) cannot call it infinite; and those who deny his existence cannot call it finite. If knowledge is infinite, there is no distinction between god and man, for infinite knowledge is infinite power: "Knowledge is Power [original in English]." Since God is by definition the "Supreme Being [original in English]," one who considers man omniscient is at once denying the existence of a supreme being. . . .

As for myself, I believe in the existence of god (even though I differ from most atheists in the definition of "god"), and therefore, must assert the finiteness of human knowledge. . . . My reason is as follows: man is not the creator of the great law governing the universe but merely a creature living within the universe created by a god; and man may perceive the will of god but not its reason nor its final purpose, just as we know $1 + 1 = 2$, which is a fact, not a reason. (XL, 13)

At the end of the "Mystery of Magic Squares," he calls to his god: "Oh, dear God! How I thank thee! Thou hath granted us, in place of infinite chimerical knowledge, an ability to pursue infinitely vast yet finite and reliable knowledge. With the mirror of wisdom endowed by thee, let us discover the signs of thy glorious will!" (XL, 16).

In this work, Rohan discusses mathematical principles of magic squares but concludes that *sū* ("number") is controlled by God. The Japanese word *sū* also means "destiny," "fate," and "law." It is in this nonmathematical sense that the concept of *sū* bears a pivotal significance in Rohan's thinking. *Sū* implies *sūki* ("vicissitudes of fortune") and *meisū* ("one's alloted span of life"). In many of his works, a character's life is condensed into a period of few hours or few days: Tae of "Encounter With a Skull" tells her life story in one night; Hikoemon the whaler supposedly in a few hours; the hermit Genkō of "A Sealed Letter" watches his own past in a vision; and all the phases of a man's life are displayed in an exhibit in the "Preface to Demon of Lust." This is not simply a literary device nor is it based on a common saying that man's life is but a brief dream.

The underlying principle in *sū*, as Rohan saw it, is the concept of cycle. In the cosmic philosophy of the *I ching* (*Book of Changes*), it appears as the cyclic changes and regeneration of life. To the Taoist alchemist in search of an elixir of immortality, it signifies the mysterious and limitless cycle in which cinnabar (mercuric sulfide) changes into mercury and again back into cinnabar; or mercury dissolves gold but vanishes through a heating process, leaving behind only gold.

In his scholarly discourse, "The Book of Immortality: *Ts'an-t'ung-ch'i*" (1941), Rohan discusses the historical development of Religious Taoism and speculates on the outer cinnabar (alchemical method) and the inner cinnabar (ritual and moral method) as well as the dual and interrelating yin and yang elements in the *I ching*. The title of the *Ts'an-t'ung-ch'i*, a Chinese work attributed to a Taoist philosopher Wei Po-yang (fl. 147–167), means "the Harmonious Unity of the Three Ways (of the Yellow Emperor, Lao Tzu, and the *I ching*)." The *Ts'an-t'ung-ch'i* deals primarily with the inner cinnabar, or spiritual cultivation. (A later book, the *Pao-p'u Tzu*, or *The Philosopher Who Embraces Simplicity*, by Ko Hung [253–333?], was heavily inclined toward the outer cinnabar of Taoist occultism.)[10]

In the context of the inner cinnabar, explains Rohan, mercury represents the brain—the center of spiritual functions—and lead is likened to the base for reproductive activities: as lead alloyed with mercury yields an amalgam, the human body and spirit together compose a human being, who is in turn capable of producing another life, that is, self-perpetuating. Religious Taoism, in fact, placed a certain emphasis on sexual activities as a means to achieve unity with universal forces and continuation of life. Rohan's "Instructions of an Old Profligate" was originally intended to include sections dealing specifically with *bōjutsu* ("art of the bed chamber") as an important factor in practice of love.

The "unity" means not only the synthesis of "the Taoist philosophy, occult wizardry, and the teachings of the *Book of Changes*,"[11] but also the correspondence between internal and external alchemy. Rohan elucidates how cinnabar was used in making the elixir of life, the best of which was called *kantan* ("return to cinnabar") produced through nine laborious processes. Then, he concludes:

If there is a concept of enlightenment in Confucian philosophy, it is not far removed from the concept of *kantan* ..., which means return to the original state of undifferentiated existence before and beyond life and death. The way of *kantan* enables man to gain his final destination, which is in turn his next origination. ... It is a way to acquire a new life, an external life, as in Zennist abrupt awakening or Christian faith. (XVIII, 488–89)

Kantan is an elixir of the highest efficacy in the outer cinnabar. In metaphysical terms of the inner cinnabar, furthermore, it signifies the attainment of the final spiritual state where life and death are no longer differentiated. It would correspond to the Great Ultimate in the *I ching*, the first principle from which all differentiated phenomena and all beings derive. This concept was emphasized by the Sung Neo-Confucians, such as Chu Hsi, who wrote a commentary, "Reexamination of *Ts'an-t'ung-ch'i*." Of the all-embracing, ever-changing Great Ultimate, Chu Hsi said, "Fundamentally there is only one Great Ultimate, yet each of the myriad things has been endowed with it and each in itself possesses the Great Ultimate in its entirety."[12]

Just as Rohan suggests, the *Ts'an-t'ung-ch'i* was an attempt to solve the problems of space, time, continuity, and existence by the concept of the Great Ultimate in order to find the way to achieve complete spiritual conversion. *Kantan* is in this sense equivalent, claims Rohan, to the Buddhist concept of emptiness or even entering into Nirvana itself. (The Great Ultimate is defined as the Nonultimate by the Neo-Confucian philosopher Chou Tun-yi, 1017–1073, in his *T'ai-ch'i-t'u-shuo*, or an Explanation of the Diagram of the Great Ultimate.)[13]

Shinoda Hajime admiringly calls our attention to Rohan's expansive vision condensed into an intense microcosm that is his cosmic epic,[14] in contrast to most writers in the so-called mainstream of Japanese literature who are oversensitive to time and preoccupied with capturing the passage of time. Shinoda praises Rohan for demonstrating such a powerful sense of space as to transform everything temporal into something spatial: he crystallizes into one moment all the vicissitudes, all the incidents in a drama from the beginning to the end.[15] In other words, unlike the naturalistic microscopic view of life, Rohan observed the universe through a telescope. He approached history and the world not simply as an accumulation of facts and individuals, but as a dynamic, organic whole, like a stage play or the Great Ultimate. He was a critical audience who watched a cosmic drama unfolded by a supreme being and, while enjoying the mystery, discovered the workings of fate—Heaven's Will and man's innate wish.

CHAPTER 11

Conclusion

I The "Absence of Ideals" Dispute

F ROM 1891 to 1892, the first and most celebrated of the Japanese literary disputes of modern times took place between two critic-novelists, Tsubouchi Shōyō and Mori Ōgai. Known as the "Absence of Ideals" dispute (*botsu risō ronsō*), the argument focused on three major issues: ideals inherent in nature; ideals reflected in art; and ideals as the criteria in artistic performance and aesthetic judgment. Despite mutual semantic misunderstanding and personal sarcasm that at times obscured the central issues, this dispute undeniably contributed enormously to clarifying the aims of modern Japanese literature and stimulating interest in literary methodology.

The preliminaries began with a series of articles by Shōyō carried by the *Yomiuri* between December, 1890, and June, 1891. In reviewing the latest short stories, Shōyō classified fiction into three categories: (1) the plot-centered—characters are provided merely to maintain some semblance of continuity unifying various incidents and coincidences (for example, the late Tokugawa romances); (2) the sentiment-centered—incidents are devices to illustrate particular human emotions without any cause-and-effect relationships between characters and incidents (for example, most of the contemporary Meiji fiction); and (3) the individual-oriented—the personality traits of a character are the primary cause of an incident, which in turn induces his next action, leading up to a climax and an eventual denouement (for example, Shakespeare).

While the plot-centered stories illustrate generalized concepts (such as loyalty, justice, wisdom) and the sentiment-centered group deals with distinctive emotions, an individual-oriented work would be modest in scale but grand in spirit, a single manifestation of multitudinous truths, particular on the surface yet universal in essence. Shōyō further declared that in opposition to dogmatic deductive criticism, he would propose an inductive approach applying a separate set of criteria to each of the three categories.

In response to this literary manifesto, Mori Ōgai published in his own magazine, *Shigarami-zōshi*, in September, 1891, a confutation based on the aesthetic theory of a German philosopher, Eduard von Hartmann (1842–1906), best known for his *Philosophy of the Unconscious* (1868). Ōgai drew a parallel between Shōyō's three categories and Hartmann's three classes of beauty: generalities or the commonplace, particularities or the individualistic, and the microcosm (*Mikrokosmismus* in German). While Shōyō conceived his categories as separate but equal, Ōgai ranked the microcosm highest in an aesthetic scale ranging from simple to complex, and superficial to profound. In addition, he refuted Shōyō's inductive, "unidealistic" criticism and advocated deductive criticism based on unequivocal criteria and ideals (aesthetic concepts).

The main contest was fought through a succession of articles appearing in *Waseda Bungaku* (Shōyō's stronghold) and *Shigarami-zōshi*. To elucidate his "unidealistic" stand, Shōyō maintained that Shakespeare's works resembled nature in providing infinite possibilities for multilevel interpretations and that he would not presume to impose his own ideals in judging such works of "panidealism." He denounced the attempt of dogmatic idealists "to apply petty ideals in measuring the macrocosm" and asserted that the function of literature was to supply the material for inductive reasoning. Ōgai retorted that in emphasizing will (nonreason) and the conscious (*Bewusstsein*), Shōyō failed to recognize reason (*Vernunft*) and the unconscious, in which exist, believed Ōgai, the concept of beauty and its ultimate perfection—the ideal of beauty.

Shōyō then apologized for his inexact use of the phrase "absence of ideals" (*botsu risō*), and explained that the absence did not imply a fundamental lack of ideal but rather "relinquishment of ideal." He refused to concur with Ōgai's belief in the existence of the Absolute Ideal and in the unconscious as the source of the ideals for a writer. Shōyō was promptly counterattacked by Ōgai, who insisted that Shōyō's relinquishing of ideals was in effect a negation of the Absolute that was Nature—a logical impossibility—and that for a writer, it would mean abandoning his creative originality, individuality, and artistic purpose. The exchanges concluded with Shōyō's proposal of truce expressed by means of a number of parodies and Ōgai's sarcastic final response in June, 1892.

To summarize this dispute, Shōyō's position was objective realism—the suppression of subjective views by the writer, and the exercise of objective judgment by the literary critic. This reflects his practical attitude and his faith in the analytical, inductive objectivism of the natural sciences. In regard to aesthetic judgment, however, this stand was a backward step from his own *Essence of the Novel*, which in effect endorsed the individual-oriented novel as his ideal, rejecting plot-centered unrealistic romances. Far from being antirealism, Ōgai's argument emphasized aesthetic value judgment in accordance with distinct standards of beauty (the ideal), for he believed that even objectively realistic (unidealistic) works could not fail to reflect the individual author's ideals.

According to von Hartmann, "the aesthetic judgment is an empirically established judgment, but has its foundation in aesthetic feeling, whose origination falls entirely within the Unconscious."[1] Since one cannot will without willing something, the content or the idea as an object of the will is essential to the will's existence. In what von Hartmann calls concrete monism, will (similar to instinct) and idea (a function of reason) are united in the Absolute Unconscious, which is the essence of the world and the principle of individuation, multiplicity, and substantiality of things.[2] Hence, Ōgai deemed Shōyō's absence of ideals to be self-contradictory both psychologically and metaphysically.

Von Hartmann distinguishes various levels of artistic production: a piece of work fails to attain the status of art if it is composed entirely of familiar elements obtainable simply by means of sense perception and a retentive memory. The ordinary talent on the next level can *idealize* through *rational selection* and combination guided by his aesthetic judgment to create a work of art that still falls short of being original.

Finally, inspired by the divine frenzy, the vivifying breath of
the unconscious, the genius attains "a unity so perfect that it
can only be compared to natural organisms, which likewise
spring out of the Unconscious."[3] Inasmuch as the microcosm,
which Ōgai identified as the highest class of literary production,
represents a unity of the concrete and the ideal, the critic must
of necessity take into consideration both the content and the
ideal reflected in a creative work of art.

The unidealism dispute is ineluctably relevant to the study
of Kōda Rohan's idealism. At three points, Ōgai mentions Rohan
as the only other writer-critic sharing the same belief in what
is equivalent to von Hartmann's microcosm as the ultimate
aesthetic ideal. In fact, Tanaka Seijirō in his article on this
dispute (*Gunzō*, May, 1954) even ventures to claim that
Ōgai's entire stand was taken in support of Rohan's idealistic
works of fiction and literary criticism. From November, 1891,
to March, 1892, throughout the heated stages of the dispute,
Rohan's best and most idealistic work, "The Five-storied
Pagoda," was serialized in the newspaper *Kokkai*, enjoying
enormous popularity and critical acclaim.

Both for their literary criticism and works of fiction, Ōgai
and Rohan are accorded the unique distinction of being the
sole members of the "Idealistic School" in modern Japanese
literature. Rohan and Ōgai are unique not only for their lofty
vision and ethical humanism but, more inexorably, because
Japanese literature developed, not in the tradition of the
microcosm or the individual-oriented novel, but regrettably in
the direction of the particularities and the sentiment-centered
approach, leaning toward the peculiarly Japanese genre of "I-
novel," sacrificing the universals in favor of the personal.

II *A Historical Perspective*

Given the present decline of Japanese naturalism and repudiation of naturalistic criticism, which had fostered the morbid
obsession with particularities, it is now time to reexamine and
reevaluate the Idealistic School, which helped prevent the tone
of Japanese literature from becoming hopelessly trivial and
vulgar. Although classed together because of their idealistic

propensity, Rohan and Ōgai are nevertheless inimitable and independent even of each other: they had neither direct predecessors nor followers to form a "school" or a group. While Ōgai was primarily indebted to German aesthetics and romanticism as well as to Japanese classical traditions, Rohan synthesized Buddhism, Christianity, Confucianism, Taoism, Chinese and Japanese literary traditions, and even natural sciences, into his own form of humanistic idealism.

Rohan's standing in modern literary history may be summed up in a few words: a grand antithesis. Rather than representing modern Japanese literature, he signified the ideal that his age could have attained both in literature and society. Early Meiji literature was dominated by prose, Western concepts, realistic techniques, objectivism, descriptions of phenomena, and mundane settings. In direct contrast, Rohan's works offer intensely poetic tone and style, Oriental transcendentalism, idealistic plot and characterization, humanistic individualism, visions of inner reality, and realms of imagination and mystery. Rohan's literary idiosyncrasies, which place him outside of the dominant currents of Japanese literature, paradoxically make his works relevant to and reflective of his contemporary society. Alone among the alienated, self-destructive, cynical, and superfluous heroes of Japanese literature, Rohan's positive, idealistic, and active hero typifies the fiery vitality and constructive idealism of early Meiji society.

Rohan's distinction is attributable also to the transitional nature of his works: the last bloom of Japanese classical traditions and the early budding of Japanese romanticism and symbolism. His view of love as spiritual, religious, aesthetic inspiration exerted crucial influence on the romantic literary group associated with the magazine, *Bungakukai* (1893–1898), which boasted such diverse types of writers as Kitamura Tōkoku, Shimazaki Tōson, and Higuchi Ichiyō. Rohan's transcendental humanism provided an initial impetus to their attempt to liberate humanity from the vulgar confines of reality.

As Okazaki Yoshie observed, furthermore, Rohan's symbolism is echoed in the symbolist poems of Kanbara Ariake (1876–1952), the plays of Kinoshita Mokutarō (1885–1945), and the symbolic short stories of Akutagawa Ryūnosuke (1892–1927), though they failed to achieve the masculine demonic force of Rohan's visions.[4]

Notes and References

References for Rohan's works are given in the text of this book without footnotes. The volume (in Roman numerals) and page number refer to *The Complete Works of Rohan* (*Rohan Zenshū* [Tokyo: Iwanami Shoten, 1950–1958]).

Japanese names are written surname first.

Chapter One

1. Thomas C. Smith, *The Agrarian Origins of Modern Japan* (Stanford, 1965).

2. Kōda Aya, "Misokkasu," in *Koda Aya Shū* (Tokyo, 1947), p. 13.

3. Yanagida Izumi, *Kōda Rohan* (Tokyo, 1942), p. 4.

4. Uemura Masahisa was professor of Meiji Gakuin Seminary, founder of numerous churches, founder and editor of *Fukuin Shinpō* (*Gospel News*), compiler and translator of hymns, and famous preacher. Among the literary figures baptized by Uemura are Kunikida Doppo (1891) and Masamune Hakuchō (1897).

5. Quoted in Yanagida Izumi, p. 6.

6. *Shashin Zusetsu Sōgō Nihonshi* (Tokyo, 1956), VI, 454–55.

7. Miyake Setsurei, *Dōjidaishi* (Tokyo, 1950), II, 506–507.

8. Shionoya San, *Kōda Rohan* (Tokyo, 1968), III, 236.

9. Gunji's funeral is the setting for *Black Kimono* (*Kuroi Suso*), a story by Rohan's daughter, Aya. His nephew Takagi Taku wrote a biography, *Gunji Shigetada Taii* (Seikatsu-sha, 1945).

10. Luther Whiting Mason (1828–1896), an American, was instructor at the Ministry of Education Music Research Center from 1880 to 1882. Komiya Toyotaka, *Japanese Music and Drama in the Meiji Era*, tr. Edward Seidensticker and Donald Keene (Tokyo, 1956), pp. 470–75.

11. Mori Ōgai, "Seigaku to Kōda-shi to," *Ōgai Zenshū* 13 (Tokyo, 1936), 302.

12. Komiya, p. 488.

13. Andō Kōko, "Andō Kō Geidan," *Rohan Zenshū Geppō*, no. 26 (1954), 2.

14. *Bundan Jiken-shi* (Tokyo, 1968).

15. Shigetomo wrote an autobiography, *Bonjin no Hanshō* (Kyōrit-

su Shobō, 1948); his academic writings have been published as *Kōda Shigetomo Chosaku Shū* (Chūō Kōron-sha, 1971).

16. See "Oku Yasutsugu no Kō" in Shōyō's miscellany, "Kaki no Heta."

17. In view of the *sodoku* training which dispensed entirely with Chinese sounds, I hesitate to speculate that Rohan's pseudonym was meant to correlate to Rakan (arhat) through their assonant Chinese pronunciation, *lu ban*.

18. Naka Arata, *Meiji no Kyōiku* (Tokyo, 1967), pp. 133–79.

19. Kōda Rohan, "Shōnen Jidai," *Konsei Shōnen* 1 (1900), 134.

20. Yanagita Kunio, *Teihon Yanagita Kunio Shū* (1964), XXX, 252.

21. Chizuka Reisui, "Geigijuku Jidai no Kōda Rohan," *Bungaku* 6 (June, 1938), 111.

22. For the life and numerous works of Satō Issai, see Takebayashi Kan'ichi, *Kangakusha Denki Shūsei* (Seki Shoin, 1945), pp. 1016–37; and an extensive entry by a philosopher friend of Rohan's, Inoue Tetsujirō, in *Shinsen Dai-jimmei Jiten* (Heibon-sha, 1940), III, pp. 108–109.

23. Kōda Rohan, "Meiji Nijū-nen Zengo no Ni-bunsei," *Waseda Bungaku* (June, 1925), 2.

24. For the significance and contents of *Shōsetsu Shinzui*, see Marleigh Ryan, *Japan's First Modern Novel: Ukigumo* (New York, 1967).

25. The Japan Railway Corporation's Tokyo-Aomori route was not open beyond Kōriyama at the time; the entire line was completed in 1891. See Okano Yukihide, "A Century of Transport Policies," *The Wheel Extended* 2 (Winter, 1972–1973), 5.

26. See *Tamagawa Hyakka Daijiten* (Tokyo, 1963), XII, 420.

27. Kangetsu first studied English and wished to become an American citizen. To forearm himself with a knowledge of Japanese culture, he began to study native literature and discovered Saikaku. He showed a tendency to shift from Zen to art, to archaeology, Christianity, to Darwinism, materialism, socialism, etc. For his life, see Rohan's "Awashima Kangetsu" (XXX, 265–70); and "Awashima Kangetsu no Koto" (XXX, 492–95).

28. Masamune Hakuchō, *Bundan Jinbutsu Hyōron* (Tokyo, 1932), p. 317.

29. Higuchi Ichiyō, *Ichiyō Zenshū* (Tokyo, 1963), IV, 297.

30. Yanagida, *Kōda Rohan*, appendices, p. 8.

31. Rohan's disciples and admirers organized an association called Kagyū-kai, which edited and published *Rohan Zenshū* after his death. Rohan often used Kagyū-an as his pseudonym.

32. A sentimental novel by Tamura Toshiko (wife of Shōgyo), "Miira no Kuchibeni," *Nihon Gendai Bungaku Zenshū* 42 (Tokyo, 1966), 214–40, has a description of Kimiko's funeral, at which Rohan is depicted as being in tears and near collapse.

33. Kimiko's tomb stands next to Rohan's, which Rohan designed himself. They are located behind the five-storied pagoda in Ikegami Honmonji, an eminent Nichiren Sect temple (designated a national treasure by the Japanese government). See Noda Utarō, *Album: Tokyo Bungaku Sanpo*, no. 45 (1954).

34. *Black Kimono* is translated by Edward Seidensticker in *Modern Japanese Short Stories* (Tokyo, 1960).

35. A short novel by Satō Haruo, *A House of Bats* (*Kōmori no Ie* [Tokyo, 1955]), is set at the ruins of Rohan's summer house at Mt. Asama in Shinshū, Yayoko's hometown. Its main character is supposed to be a distant relative of Yayoko, and the plot unfolds around the unsavory rumors that Yayoko had been a fallen woman until Rohan delivered her from a brothel by marrying her. Satō mentions Rohan and Yayoko by name, but the story is mostly unfounded conjecture and imagination. In truth, Rohan and Yayoko were married by Uemura Masahisa in church.

36. Kōda Aya, "Misokkasu," p. 39.

37. Ibid., p. 47.

38. Mushakōji Saneatsu, *Rohan Zenshū Geppō*, no. 3 (1949), 6.

39. Kōda Aya, "Shūen," p. 259.

Chapter Two

1. Kenyūsha's fiction magazine was called *Garakuta Bunko* from May, 1885, to January, 1889; and simply *Bunko* for February to October, 1889.

2. For a detailed discussion of Meiji literary styles, see Ryan.

3. Yoda Gakkai, "Gakkai Nichiroku," *Rohan Zenshū Geppō*, no. 20 (1952), 1.

4. William Makepeace Thackeray (1811–1863); and Edward George Earle Bulwer-Lytton (1803–1873), whose *Ernest Maltravers* (1837) was translated into Japanese by Niwa Jun'ichirō as *Karyū Shunwa* in 1878 and enjoyed critical acclaim as well as wide popularity.

5. Uchida Roan, "Rohan no Shussebanashi," *Rohan Zenshū Geppō*, no. 3 (1949), 12.

6. Tayama Katai, "Tokyo no Sanjū-nen," *Gendai Nihon Bungaku Zenshū* 97 (Tokyo, 1958), 288.

7. Masaoka Shiki, "Tennōji-han no Kagyū-an," *Shiki Zenshū* 14, (Tokyo, 1912), 752–53.

8. For Rohan's style, see Hiraoka Toshio, "Kōda Rohan," *Koku-bungaku Kaishaku to Kanshō* (January, 1969), 67–72; and Naruse Masakatsu, "Rohan no Buntai," *Bungaku* (August, 1940), 44–48.

Chapter Three

1. Shimada Kinji, *Kindai Hikaku Bungaku* (Tokyo, 1956), pp. 181–82.

2. William Edward Soothill, *The Lotus of the Wonderful Law* (London, 1930), p. 60.

3. Ōchō Enichi, *Hokke Shisō* (Kyoto, 1969), pp. 97–98.

4. Nichiren, *Nichiren Shōnin Ibun* (Kyoto, 1965), II, 1541–42.

5. Soothill, p. 174.

6. Nichiren, "Kaimoku-shō," *Nichiren Shōnin Ibun Daikōza* 2 (Tokyo, 1967), 377.

7. Donald Keene, ed., "Dōjōji," in *Twenty Plays of the Nō Theatre* (New York, 1970), p. 251.

8. Kitamura Tōkoku's short story, "My Prison" (*Waga Rōgoku*, 1893), is inspired by "Enlightenment of Love" and deals with the same theme. Tōkoku's protagonist, however, finds no solace in his prison of love, fundamentally suffering from the Christian sense of guilt and skepticism of modern man.

9. Kino Kazuyoshi, "Bosatsu-gyō," in *Hokke Shisō*, ed. Ōchō Enichi (Kyoto, 1969), p. 428.

10. Tamura Shōgyo, "Shin Hagoromo Monogatari no Koro," *Rohan Zenshū Geppō*, no. 16 (1951), 9.

Chapter Four

1. *Rohan no Shokan*, ed. Kōda Aya (Tokyo, 1951), p. 15.

2. The tea cult in Japan was actively promoted by Zen Buddhism, which supplied religious significance for the setting of the tea ceremony: the exterior of the tea hut was equated with the evanescence of all things; the garden with the selflessness of all elements; the hut's interior with the bliss of Nirvana, where the smoke of incense symbolized the constant aspiration of the terrestrial toward the celestial (*jōgubodai*). See William de Bary, *Sources of Japanese Tradition* (New York, 1958), I, 257–60.

3. Okazaki Yoshie, *Fūryū no Shisō: Nihon Geijutsu Shichō* (Tokyo, 1948), II, 28.

4. *Rohan no Shokan*, p. 18.

5. Mibu Daishun, *Hannya Shin-gyō* (Tokyo, 1971), p. 139.

6. Frederick Streng, *Emptiness: A Study in Religious Meaning* (New York, 1967), p. 169.

7. Kino Kazuyoshi, *Inochi no Sekai: Hokke-kyō* (Tokyo, 1965), pp. 131–32.

8. Kobayashi Ichirō, *Hokke-kyō Daikōza* (Tokyo, 1965), VIII, 299.

Chapter Five

1. Gotō Chūgai, "Bimyō, Kōyō, Rohan no San-sakka o Hyō-su," *Meiji Bungaku Zenshū* 25 (1968), 387.

2. The poet Kitahara Hakushū (1885–1942), who around 1926 resided on the same street as did a number of other writers, was also inspired by this pagoda to write poems such as: "Oh, the Pagoda! / Beautiful is the curve of your five roofs, / This lovely spring noon, / Against the floating white clouds." "Tennō-ji Bohan Gin," *Nihon no Bungaku* 17 (Tokyo, 1968), 186.

3. Tsubouchi Shōyō, "Shōsetsu Obanashū," *Waseda Bungaku*, no. 28 (1892), 25.

4. The two characters for Rohan's real name (Shigeyuki) have an alternate reading, Nariyuki, which does not apply in his case.

5. Seki Ryōichi, "Kōyō, Rohan, Ichiyō," *Kōza Nihon Bungaku* 9 (Tokyo, 1969), 68–80.

6. Yamazaki Yasuo, *Iwanami Bunko o Meguru Bungō Hiwa* (Tokyo, 1965), p. 77. Rohan was particularly closely associated with the Iwanami Publishing Company, through the devotion of Iwanami's son-in-law and executive, Kobayashi Isamu.

7. Shionoya, II, 205–208.

8. Kōda Aya, "Otōto," pp. 194–95.

9. Fukuda Kiyoto, *Kenyūsha no Bungaku Undō* (Tokyo, 1950), pp. 116–17.

Chapter Six

1. Kitamura Tōkoku, "Karamakura oyobi Shin-Hazue-shū ni tsuite," *Tōkoku Zenshū* 1 (Tokyo, 1963), 279.

2. Yanagida Izumi, "Kōro Jidai," *Bungaku* 6 (June, 1938), 83.

3. William Theodore de Bary, *Self and Society in Ming Thought* (New York, 1970), p. 4.

4. Ibid., p. 151.

5. Marius Jansen, "The Meiji State: 1868–1912," *Modern East Asia*, James B. Crowly, ed. (New York, 1970), 117.

6. Itō Sei, "Rohan o Chūshin ni," *Bungaku* 26 (July, 1958), 128–29.

7. Refer to Irokawa Daikichi, *Meiji Seishinshi* (Tokyo, 1968), 270–71.

164 KŌDA ROHAN

8. See Kataoka Ryōichi, "Rohan no Rinkaku," *Bungaku* 15 (October, 1947), 62.

9. Shimada, pp. 115–16.

10. George Woods and Jerome Buckley, eds., *Poetry of the Victorian Period* (New York, 1955), p. 1011.

11. Walter J. Bate, ed., *Criticism: The Major Texts* (New York, 1952), p. 508.

12. Ishida Mizumaro, *Jissen no Michi: Hannya, Yuima-kyō* (Tokyo, 1965), p. 198.

13. Kitagawa Momoo, "Kangaden," *Rohan Zenshū Geppō*, no. 7 (1949), 9.

14. Kino Kazuyoshi, "Bosatsu-gyō," pp. 424–52.

15. Kobayashi, IV, 123–203.

16. de Bary, *Sources of Japanese Tradition*, I, 148.

17. Ibid., II, 74.

18. Murakami Yoshizane, *Chūgoku no Sennin* (Kyoto, 1956), p. 1.

19. Kobayashi, VIII, 286–330.

20. "Benzai Tennyo," *Rohan Zenshū*, XXXI, 321–23.

21. Soothill, p. 1.

22. Ibid., p. 157.

23. Hendrik Kern, *Saddharma-Pundarika: The Lotus of the True Law* (New York, 1963), p. 230, note 1.

24. Akizuki Ryōmin, ed., *Rinzairoku* (Tokyo, 1972), p. 101.

25. Tsubouchi, "Shōsetsu Obana-shū," p. 25.

26. Honma Hisao, *Meiji Bungakushi* (Tokyo, 1935), II, 229–30.

27. Henrik Ibsen, *Ibsen*, trans. James Walter McFarlene (New York, 1972), p. 250.

28. Irving Deer, "Ibsen's *Brand*: Paradox and the Symbolic Hero," in *Ibsen*, ed. Rolf Fjelde (Englewood Cliffs, 1965), p. 58.

29. William Ernest Hocking, "A Brief Note on Individual in East and West," in *The Status of the Individual in East and West*, ed. Charles A. Moore (Honolulu, 1968), p. 94.

30. de Bary, *Self and Society in Ming Thought*, p. 20.

31. Murakami, p. 6.

32. Tashiro Jinki, ed., *Chūshaku Hagakure* (Tokyo, 1942), p. 7.

33. Nakamura Hajime, *Jihi* (Kyoto, 1968), p. 221.

34. Araki Kōjirō, "Nichiren-shū ni okeru Jōgyō Bosatsudō," in *Daijō Bosatsudō no Kenkyū*, ed. Nishi Yoshio (Kyoto, 1968), p. 597.

Chapter Seven

1. Zola was introduced to Japan through English editions around 1888. Kōyō's "A Woodsman's Love" (1889), on which Rohan wrote

Notes and References

165

a review, is directly inspired by Zola's *La Faute de l'Abbe Mouret* (1875).

2. Shinoda Hajime, *Sakuhin ni tsuite* (Tokyo, 1971), pp. 94–95.

3. Donald Keene, *Anthology of Japanese Literature* (New York, 1955), p. 314.

4. Kōda Rohan, "Rohan Dansō-shō," *Kokugo to Kokubungaku* 11 (August, 1934), 81–95.

5. The figures are from Yanagida Izumi, *Kōda Rohan*, p. 211.

6. *The Minute Storehouse of Life* influenced Higuchi Ichiyō's best work, "Growing Up" (1895–1896).

7. For Indra's net, see Garma C. C. Chang, *The Buddhist Teaching of Totality: The Philosophy of Hwa Yen Buddhism* (University Park, 1971), p. 165.

8. Wm. Theodore de Bary, *Sources of Chinese Tradition* (New York, 1964), pp. 329–33.

9. Suetsuna Joichi, *Kegon-gyō no Sekai* (Tokyo, 1967), p. 20.

10. Ibid., p. 24.

11. Ibid., p. 60.

12. Ibid., p. 66.

13. Naruse Masakatsu, "Kōyō to Rohan ni okeru Shōsetsu no Rinen," *Kokubungaku Kaishaku to Kanshō* 31 (January, 1966), 24.

14. *Jijoron* probably refers to Samuel Smiles' *Self Help*, which was translated into Japanese by Nakamura Masanao as *Saigoku Risshi Hen* (*Success Stories of the West*) in 1870–1871. Rohan cited this book among the recommended readings for self-cultivation. (The others were the *Analects*, *Mencious*, Old and New Testaments, Sontoku's *Hōtokuki*, and Wang Yang-ming's *Ch'uan-hsi-lu*.) (XL, 693)

15. Murakami, p. 214.

16. Kobayashi, V, 90.

17. Hirano Sōjō, ed., *Tongo Yōmon* (Tokyo, 1970), p. 176.

18. Akizuki, p. 102.

19. Saitō Mokichi, *Saitō Mokichi Zenshū*, V, 469.

Chapter Eight

1. In the issues from no. 8 to no. 31, this column was renamed *Unchūgo* (*Talks in the Clouds*), with additional panel members, including Ozaki Kōyō and Yoda Gakkai.

2. Saitō Ryokuu (1867–1904) was novelist, critic, essayist, known for biting satire, humorous yet cynical parody, and poignant insight. He died of consumption after posting his own obituary in the newspapers.

3. *Shin Shōsetsu* (July, 1896–November, 1926) made invaluable

contributions to modern Japanese literature, publishing ambitious works such as Sōseki's *The Three-cornered World* (1906), Tayama Katai's *Futon* (1907), Nagai Kafū's *Sumida River* (1909), Akutagawa's *Yum Gruel* (1916), and numerous others.

4. Tashiro, p. 12.

5. Furukawa Tesshi, "The Individual in Japanese Ethics," in *The Status of the Individual in East and West*, ed. Charles A. Moore (Honolulu, 1968), p. 301.

6. Tashiro, p. 12.

7. *The Sorrows of Young Werther* was at first read in Gotzberg's loose English translation (1802, the Cassell's National Library edition), which placed distorted emphasis on pessimistic sentimentalism. A partial translation in Japanese appeared in 1889 (in *Kokumin no Tomo* and in *Shin Shōsetsu*) and 1894 (in *Shigarami-zōshi*), prior to a complete translation of 1904.

8. Kobayashi, VII, 355.

9. Ibid., VIII, 462–76.

10. This story is depicted in the painting on the famous Tamamushi Shrine in the Hōryūji Temple.

11. Saitō, XXXIX, 294. Mokichi admired "This Day" so much that he entitled his first collection of poems *Shakkō* (*Crimson Glow*) and chose "Shakkō-in" for his own posthumous Buddhist name, after the crimson glow into which the emperor's spirit vanishes.

12. Rohan used to play a unique family game with his children at relaxed moments. They would converse in a certain chosen way, such as simulating Tokugawa speech or using as many foreign words as possible. (His daughter Aya was sent to a Christian school where English was taught by Western instructors.) Aya recalls that her father was always the winner, but once when he was speaking in the samurai language, she began to retort in the Tokugawa courtesan diction; it made Rohan so uncomfortable that he suggested they switch to the *Tale of Genji* style, and Aya was finally beaten in the difficult Heian syntax, which Rohan manipulated with ease. Kōda Aya, "Chigiregumo," in *Kōda Aya Shū*, p. 267.

Chapter Nine

1. Shionoya, I, 434.

2. "Rohan Dansōshō," p. 38.

3. Ibid., pp. 88–90.

4. Ibid., p. 91.

5. Friedrich Nietzsche, *Thus Spake Zarathustra*, trans. Thomas Common (New York, 1964), p. 191.

6. For Nietzsche in Japan, see Tezuka Tomio, *Niiche* (Tokyo, 1966), p. 53.

7. Kino, *Inochi no Sekai: Hokke-gyō*, p. 17.

8. Kobayashi, VII, 356.

9. Kino, p. 17.

10. Ōchō, p. 58.

11. Seri Hiroaki, *Bunmei Hihyōka to shite no Rohan* (Tokyo, 1971), p. 280.

12. Tsuchida Kyōson, *Shōchō no Tetsugaku* (Kyoto, 1948), p. 42.

13. Kōda Rohan, *Leaving the Hermitage* (London, 1925), p. 9.

Chapter Ten

1. de Bary, *Sources of Chinese Tradition*, I, 32.

2. Ibid., p. 33.

3. Tanizaki Junichirō, "Jōzetsuroku," *Tanizaki Junichirō Zenshū* 20 (Tokyo, 1968), 164–65.

4. Ibid., p. 165.

5. Shinoda Hajime, *Sakuhin ni tsuite*, p. 65.

6. Usui Yoshimi, *Ningen to Bungaku* (Tokyo, 1957), p. 178.

7. Funayama Shinichi, *Meiji Tetsugakushi Kenkyū* (Tokyo, 1959), pp. 173–74.

8. Ibid., p. 181.

9. Uemura Masahisa, "Shinri Ippan," *Uemura Masahisa Chosakushū* 4 (Tokyo, 1966), 50–108.

10. de Bary, *Sources of Chinese Tradition*, I, 256–57.

11. Ibid., p. 257.

12. Ibid., p. 484.

13. Ibid., p. 458.

14. Shinoda Hajime, "Kōda Rohan no tame ni," *Bungaku* 34 (May, 1966), 21.

15. Shinoda, *Sakuhin ni tsuite*, pp. 85–86.

Chapter Eleven

1. Eduard von Hartmann, *Philosophy of the Unconscious* (New York, 1931), I, 274–75.

2. Dennis Darnoi, *The Unconscious and Eduard von Hartmann* (The Hague, 1967), pp. 55–59.

3. von Hartmann, p. 279.

4. Okazaki Yoshie, "Rohan no Unmeikan," *Geirin Kanpo* (July-August, 1947), 59.

Selected Bibliography

PRIMARY SOURCES

1. In Japanese

Rohan no Shokan. Edited by Kōda Aya. Tokyo: Kōbun-dō, 1951.
Rohan Zenshū. Tokyo: Iwanami Shoten, 1950–1958.

The following are the titles of Rohan's works mentioned in the text. All of them are included in *Rohan Zenshū.*

Ayashi yana. (How Suspicious!)
Dogū Mokugū. (Clay Image, Wooden Image.)
Dokushushin. (Venomous Coral Lips.)
Doryokuron. (On Endeavor.)
Etsuraku. (On Joy and Pleasure.)
Fūjibumi. (A Sealed Letter.)
Fūryūbutsu. (Love Bodhisattva.)
Fūryū Enmaden. (Instructions of an Old Profligate.)
Fūryūgo. (Enlightenment of Love.)
Fūryūma. (The Demon of Love.)
Fūryūmajo. (Preface to the Demon of Love.)
Fūryū Mijinzō. (The Minute Storehouse of Life.)
    1. *Sasabune.* (Bamboo-leaf Boats.)
    2. *Usurai.* (Thin Ice.)
    3. *Tsuyukusa.* (Dayflowers.)
    4. *Teitetsu.* (Horseshoes.)
    5. *Nibasakazuki.* (The Lotus-leaf Cup.)
    6. *Kiku no Hamamatsu.* (Beach Pines of Kiku.)
    7. *Sannaki-guruma.* (The Small-wheeled Cart.)
    8. *Agarigama.* (A Useless Sickle.)
    9. *Miyakodori.* (Seagulls.)
Fūryū Zentenma. (Secular Zen, the Arch Demon.)
Futsuka Monogatari. (Tales of Two Days.)
    Kono Ichinichi. (This Day.)
    Kano Ichinichi. (That Day.)
Gojū no Tō. (The Five-storied Pagoda.)
Hakugan Daruma. (A Blank-eyed Daruma.)

Hana no Iroiro. (Catalogue of Flowers.)
Hannya Shin-gyō Dai-nigi Chū. (Commentary on the Secondary Meaning of the Heart Sutra.)
Haru no Yogatari. (Spring Night's Tale.)
Higeotoko. (A Bearded Man.)
Hōjin Hisetsu. (Mystery of Magic Squares.)
Honbako Taiji. (Conquest of Bookcases.)
Ikkōken. (A Sword.)
Isanatori. (The Whaler.)
Isei-hen. (Commentry on "Government.")
Ishana no Sono. (Iśāna's Garden.)
Issetsuna. (One Instant.)
Kaidan. (Supernatural Tales.)
Kangadan. (Viewing of a Painting.)
Kekkōsei. (The Blood-red Star.)
Kidanji. (A Rare Man.)
Kokkeidan. (Humorous Stories.)
Konsei Mafū. (Evil Wind in the Chaotic World.)
Kore wa, Kore wa. (Surprise!)
Kottō. (Antiques.)
Kumo no Iroiro. (Catalogue of Clouds.)
Meian Futaomote. (Dark Side, Bright Side.)
Nemimi Deppō. (Surprise Gunshot.)
Nihonka. (A Song of Japan.)
Nogi Shōgun. (General Nogi.)
Oto to Kotoba. (Sound and Words.)
Renkanki. (Records of Linked Rings.)
Rikyū no Tsuma. (Rikyū's Wife.)
Sensho Sandōkei. (Book of Immortality: *Ts'an-t'ung-ch'i.*)
Shin Bijin. (True Beauty.)
Shin Urashima. (New Urashima.)
Shumi. (On Taste.)
Shutsuro. (Leaving the Hermitage.)
Sora Utsu Nami. (Waves Dashing Against Heaven.)
Suijō Goi. (Vocabulary of the Water.)
Taidokuro. (Encounter with a Skull.)
Tarōbō. (A Saké Cup.)
Tetsu no Kitae. (Tempering of Iron.)
Tokkan Kikō. (Journal of a Desperate Journey.)
Tsuji Jōruri. (The Wandering Balladeer.)
Tsuyu Dandan. (Dewdrops.)
Umi to Nihonbungaku to. (The Ocean and Japanese Literature.)
Unmei. (Destiny.)

Waen. (A Garden of Tales.)
Wankyū Monogatari. (Kyūbei the Potter.)
Yūjin. (Floating Dust.)
Yuki Funpun. (Snowflakes Dancing.)

2. In English

Leaving the Hermitage. Translated by Nagura Jirō. London: George Allen and Unwin, 1925.
"Lodging for the Night." In *Representative Tales of Japan.* Translated by Miyamori Asataro. Tokyo: Sansei-dō, 1914.
The Pagoda. Translated by Shioya Sakae. Tokyo: Ōkura Shoten, 1909.

SECONDARY SOURCES

The following list includes only the materials which relate directly to Rohan and his works and which have been of greatest help to my research effort.

ABE TAIGO. *Bukkyō to Bungaku no Hiroba.* Tokyo: Hyakkaen, 1959. A Buddhist scholar's discussion of philosophical concepts reflected in Rohan's fiction.
AKAGI KENSUKE. "Rohan no Shōsetsu." In *Nihon no Shōsetsu.* Edited by Inagaki Tatsurō. Tokyo: Tōdai Shuppan Kai, 1957. A historical perspective.
CHIZUKA REISUI. "Geigijuku Jidai no Kōda Rohan." *Bungaku* 6 (June, 1938), 106–16. A friend's recollections of their student days.
FUKUMOTO KAZUO. *Nihon Runessansu-shiron kara Mita Kōda Rohan.* Tokyo: Hōsei Daigaku Shuppan Kyoku, 1972. A very competent, original, engrossing reevaluation of Rohan's standing in modern Japanese intellectual history.
GOTO CHŪGAI. "Bimyō, Kōyō, Rohan no San-sakka o Hyō-su." *Meiji Bungaku Zenshū* 25 (Chikuma Shobō, 1968), 367–87. An enthusiastic review of Rohan's works by a contemporary of his.
HIRAOKA TOSHIO. "Kōda Rohan," *Kokubungaku Kaishaku to Kanshō* 34 (January, 1969), 67–72. A thorough analysis of Rohan's style.
INO KENJI. "Rohan: Moo Hitotsu no Kindai." *Bungaku* 38 (October, 1970), 1–13. Reevaluation of Rohan from the post-naturalism standpoint.
ITŌ SEI. "Rohan o Chūshin ni." *Bungaku* 26 (July, 1958), 103–30. Social significance of the Rohanesque positive heroes.
IZAWA MOTOMI. "Fūryū Enmaden." *Meiji Taishō Bungaku Kenkyū* 3 (May, 1950), 119–20. Traces the processes through which "Instructions of an Old Profligate" acquired its final title.

KATAOKA RYOICHI. "Rohan no Rinkaku." *Bungaku* 15 (October, 1947), 62–72.

————. "Rohan no Tokuchō to Sono Genkai." *Kokugo to Koku-bungaku* 24 (November, 1947), 1–7. A perceptive discussion of Rohan's literary idiosyncrasies and their limitations.

————. "Shajitsushugi Sakka to shite no Rohan." *Bungaku* 6 (June, 1938), 40–61. Rohan's merits and flaws as a realist writer.

KIMURA TAKESHI. "Tatsujin no Bungaku: Kōda Rohan no Koto." *Kokubungaku Kaishaku to Kanshō* 31 (February, 1966), 157–63. A rather impressionistic consideration of Rohan as a philosophical writer.

KINOSHITA MOKUTARŌ. "Kōda Rohan." *Mokutarō Zenshū*. Tokyo: Iwanami Shoten, 1950, VII, 144–82. An aesthete poet's admiration for Rohan.

KITAMURA TŌKOKU. "Karamakura oyobi Shin-Hazueshū." *Tōkoku Zenshū*. Tokyo: Iwanami Shoten, 1963, I, 272–79. A critical review of "The Wandering Balladeer" and "Surprise Gunshot" by a romanticist poet.

MAEDA AI. "Sakka ni miru Nashonarizumu: Kōda Rohan." *Koku-bungaku Kaishaku to Kanshō* 36 (June, 1971), 45–91. Nationalism and Rohan.

MIKI KATSUMI. "Josen Gaishi to Kōda Rohan no Unmei." *Chūgoku Bungakuhō* (October, 1955), 91–128. *A Popular Biography of a Lady Mystic* and Rohan's "Destiny."

NARUSE MASAKATSU. "Kōda Rohan Ron." In *Meiji no Sakka-tachi*. Edited by Nakajima Kenzō, et al. Tokyo: Eihō-sha, 1955, 65–97. A comprehensive discussion of Rohan.

————. "Kōyō to Rohan ni okeru Shōsetsu no Rinen." *Kokubungaku Kaishaku to Kanshō* 31 (January, 1966), 20–24. A study on Rohan's concept of fiction.

————. "Rohan no Buntai." *Bungaku* 8 (August, 1940), 44–48. A stylistic analysis.

————. "Rohan to Ōgai." *Bungaku* 6 (June, 1938), 84–89. Rohan as an idealistic writer.

OKAZAKI YOSHIE. "Rohan no Unmeikan." *Geirin Kanpo* (July-August, 1947), 57–65. Rohan's concept of destiny.

SERI HIROAKI. *Bunmei Hihyōka to shite no Rohan*. Tokyo: Mirai-sha, 1971. A competent reassessment of Rohan's intellectual contributions.

————. "Kōda Rohan to Nishida Kitarō." *Bungaku: Gogaku* 35 (March, 1965), 81–90. A comparative study of Rohan's philosophical views.

————. "Rohan Bungaku ni okeru Kegon Shisō ni tsuite." *Gobun*

Kenkyū (February, 1966), 38–48. Traces the influence of the Kegon doctrine on Rohan's fiction.

SHINODA HAJIME. *Sakuhin ni Tsuite.* Tokyo: Chikuma Shobō, 1971. An insightful reappraisal and defense of Rohan.

SHIONOYA SAN. *Kōda Rohan.* Tokyo: Chūō Kōron-sha, 1965–1968. The most definitive and comprehensive biography, in three volumes, covering Rohan's personal life as well as his career, but without critical analysis.

TANAKA SEIJIRŌ. "Ōgai to Rohan." *Gunzō* 9 (May, 1954), 162–70. Somewhat dogmatically asserts that Rohan was the model for Ōgai's "idealist writer" defined in the course of the Unidealism Dispute.

TAKAO RYŌICHI. "Ōgai, Rohan to Mokichi." *Kokubungaku Kaishaku to Kanshō* 30 (April, 1965), 59–62. Rohan's impact on Saitō Mokichi.

TSUBOUCHI SHŌYŌ. "Shōsetsu Obanashū." *Waseda Bungaku,* no. 28 (1892), 25. A complimentary review of "The Five-storied Pagoda."

YAMAGUCHI TSUYOSHI. "Rohan-shi no Fūryūbutsu." *Waseda Bungaku* (April, 1926), 92–99. A discussion of "Love Bodhisattva."

YANAGIDA IZUMI. *Kōda Rohan.* Tokyo: Chūō Kōron-sha, 1942. An analytical and literary biography dealing with Rohan's early phases prolific in fiction.

————. "Kōro Jidai." *Bungaku* 6 (June, 1938), 73–83. Consideration of Rohan's significance in literary history.

Index